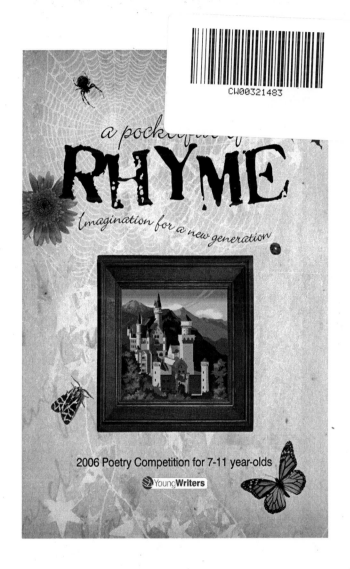

a pocketful of

RHYME

Imagination for a new generation

2006 Poetry Competition for 7-11 year-olds

YoungWriters

North West England Vol II
Edited by Young Writers

Editorial Team

Lynsey Hawkins
Allison Dowse
Claire Tupholme
Donna Samworth
Aimée Vanstone
Gemma Hearn
Angela Fairbrace
Heather Killingray
Jessica Woodbridge

 Young**Writers**
First published in Great Britain in 2006 by:
Young Writers
Remus House
Coltsfoot Drive
Peterborough
PE2 9JX
Telephone: 01733 890066
Website: www.youngwriters.co.uk

SB ISBN 1 84602 445 5

Foreword

Young Writers was established in 1991 and has been passionately devoted to the promotion of reading and writing in children and young adults ever since. The quest continues today. Young Writers remains as committed to the nurturing of poetic and literary talent as ever.

This year's Young Writers competition has proven as vibrant and dynamic as ever and we are delighted to present a showcase of the best poetry from across the UK and in some cases overseas. Each poem has been selected from a wealth of *A Pocketful Of Rhyme* entries before ultimately being published in this, our fourteenth primary school poetry series.

Once again, we have been supremely impressed by the overall quality of the entries we have received. The imagination, energy and creativity which has gone into each young writer's entry made choosing the poems a challenging and often difficult but ultimately hugely rewarding task - the general high standard of the work submitted ensured this opportunity to bring their poetry to a larger appreciative audience.

We sincerely hope you are pleased with this final collection and that you will enjoy *A Pocketful Of Rhyme North West England Vol II* for many years to come.

Contents

Duddon St Peter's CE Primary School, Tarporley

Sadie Page (10)	47
Thomas Greaves (10)	47
Harry Tomkinson (9)	48
Amy Hallam (11)	48
Matthew Magee (11)	48
Tom Okell (9)	49
Pippa Higgins (10)	49
Matthew Barge (10)	49
Rebecca Blagg (9)	50
Ben Leaman (11)	50
Helena Grantham (9)	50
Beatrice Benson (9)	51
Katie Blagg (10)	51
Kathryn Antrobus (11)	51
Hannah Willcocks (11)	52
Oliver Deakin (10)	52
Holly Jenkins (9)	52
Joe Melody Rupnik (10)	53
Abbie Mulherin (9)	53
Tom Sarstedt (10)	53
Jade Derbyshire (11)	54
Elaine Mercer (11)	54
Jack Williamson (11)	55

Fairfield Junior School, Widnes

Molly Watts (10)	55
Jade Corcoran (11)	56
Abbie Geraghty (11)	56
Liam Sheeran (11)	57
Isabelle Smith (10)	57
Chelsea Wignall (11)	58
Alison Sparks (11)	58
Alyshea O'Neill (11)	59
Jessica Wilson (10)	59
Thomas Dudley (10)	60
Chloe Jones (10)	60
Kaylee O'Brien (11)	61
Michael Matthews (10)	61
Gareth Watson (10)	62
Matthew McCormick (10)	62

Forest School, Timperley

Abigail Turner (6)	63
Connor Rutherford (6)	63
Annabel Clark (10)	64
James Proctor (11)	64
Aishwarya Bhatkhande (11)	65
Liberty Nicholls (10)	65
Andrew Clucas (11)	66
Alexandra Cupples (11)	67
Gabriella Seaton (10)	68
Phillip Murphy (10)	69
Jamil Latif (10)	70
Lucy Garratt (11)	71
Jessica Gaskell (11)	72
Sarah Nicholson (11)	73

Glazebury CE Primary School, Glazebury

Bradley Stephenson (8)	73
Ellis Carney (8)	74
Abbie Lynch (9)	74
Thomas Chadwick (8)	75
Nathaniel Pestell-Jones (8)	75
Lucy Johnson (8)	76
Grace Hindley (8)	76
Todd Edgar (8)	77
Harry Spencer (9)	77
Joe Love (9)	78
Morgan Fearnley (9)	78
Harry Love (8)	79

Golborne Community Primary School, Golborne

Jennie Richmond (9)	79
Lizzie Pilling (8)	80
Bethany Wilding (8)	80
Charlotte Govan (7)	81
Nicole Thompson (8)	81
Helen Taylor (8)	82

Halton Lodge Primary School, Runcorn

Lewis Harry (10)	82
Emma Sheakey (11)	83

Heversham St Peter's CE Primary School, Milnthorpe

Natasha Wightman (10)	83
Maria Inman (11)	84
Phillip Armstrong (8)	84
Georgia Nield (10)	85
Katherine Atkinson (11)	85
Alice Pickthall (11)	86
Megan Carling (9)	86
Jessica Pickthall (10)	87
Charlotte Thwaites-Breed (10)	87
Joanna Peers (10)	88
Zak Crosby-McCann (9)	88
Francesca Ely (8)	89
Alex Child (9)	89
Eilish Halford (11)	90
Ritchie Budd (8)	90
Elliot Handley (7)	91
Heather Wilkins (7)	91
Sophie Richards (9)	92
Holly Robinson (11)	93
Rosanna Ely (10)	94
Rachel Nield (8)	94
Sophie Watson (7)	95
George Pickthall (8)	95
Benedict Willacy (8)	95
Ed McGaulley (7) & Sam Coates (8)	96
Megan Byles (8)	96
Tara McGaulley (9)	97
Dominique Davies (8)	97
Holly Watson (9)	98

Kingsley St John's CE Primary School, Kingsley

Chloe Sproston (7)	98
Marcus Alexander Lythgoe (8)	99
Tom Waring (8)	99
Alex Daugan (9)	99
Alexander Palfreyman (8)	100
Daniel Steen (8)	100
Matthew Thomas Lythgoe (8)	100
Oliver Cartwright (7)	101
Nina Atkinson (9)	101

Monton Green Primary School, Eccles

The Poems

The Wolf

Wolf, wolf frightening sight,
Leader, follows light of the night,
Spins 'round to meet his foe
Fighting, killing the life of a doe.

Farmers search day and night,
The wolf knows all and he takes flight,
Living, stealing in a thieving light,
Telling all to be in fright,
Living, stealing, king of moonlight.

All night picking
The fattest chicken,
Farmers pay no heed to warning,
Only to find out in the morning.
Wolf, wolf shining bright,
King of the moonlight.

Akashaditya Das (11)
Chetwynde School, Barrow-in-Furness

Santa's Sack

In his sack Santa hid . . .
Ten brightly coloured scarves all cosy
Nine cuddly teddy bears
Eight knitting balls for Grandma
Seven little monkeys jumping up and down
Six pretty hair bobbles for cousin Rose
Five kittens saying *miaow*
Four jack-in-the-boxes going *boing*
Three huge barking dogs
Two colourful parrots squawking
And *one . . . guess what?*

Zanna Messenger-Jones (8)
Chetwynde School, Barrow-in-Furness

The Full Moon

The full moon,
Floating about in space,
Large, bright, scary,
Like a piece of holey cheese,
Like a crystal in the night sky,
I feel like someone is watching me,
A big, ominous presence,
The full moon,
Makes me think that there might be life on other planets.

Andrew Forster (11)
Chetwynde School, Barrow-in-Furness

The Mountain

The mountain,
Towering above everything,
Huge, giant, humungous,
Like a finger pointing at the sky,
Like a natural pyramid,
Makes me feel small,
Like a tiny ant,
The mountain.

Charlie Raine (11)
Chetwynde School, Barrow-in-Furness

The Old Tree

The old tree
Grown many thousands of years ago
Big, strong, tall
Like an elf with a tall hat on
It makes me feel like I'm looking at a giant
The old tree
Reminds me of a man crying with the tears
Floating down in the wind.

Douglas Jardine (11)
Chetwynde School, Barrow-in-Furness

The Blazing Sun

The blazing sun
Blazing, mighty, bright
Like a candle in the sky
Like a house on fire
It makes me feel happy
Like a meteor
The blazing sun
Reminds me of how young I am.

David Clafton (10)
Chetwynde School, Barrow-in-Furness

The Bluey-Green Ocean

Home to many things,
Like an everlasting watery splashy field,
Like a jungle with fish as the animals,
It makes me feel alone,
Like shells, sand and sea are the only things near me,
The bluey-green ocean
Reminds me of how old the world is.

Hannah Barry (10)
Chetwynde School, Barrow-in-Furness

The Dreamy Clouds

The dreamy clouds
Made from thousands of droplets of water
Majestic, calm, peaceful
Like a river - forever flowing
They make me feel peaceful
Like a white dove gliding
The dreamy clouds
Remind us that life keeps going
No matter what happens.

Sarah Costigan (11)
Chetwynde School, Barrow-in-Furness

Springtime

In fields there are crops,
In gardens there are snowdrops.
Outside the lambs run,
Dance below the heated sun.

The ram is with the ewe,
In the background the cows moo.
While the lambs are getting lost,
Cold in the winter's frost.

Everywhere are daffodils,
Along the snow-capped hills.
Below the sheep are bleating,
Standing around in a meeting!

Kelly Sankey (10)
Chetwynde School, Barrow-in-Furness

An Ant

An ant
It is an animal
Tiny, weak, fast
Like a tiny pebble
Like a small scorpion
Makes me annoyed
Like a TV show on antiques
An ant
Reminds me of how strong I am.

Rory Flynn (11)
Chetwynde School, Barrow-in-Furness

Santa's Sack

In his sack Santa hid . . .
Ten cats, black and brown
Nine snakes, yellow and red
Eight monkeys, black and white
Seven bears, brown
Six goldfish, orange and yellow
Five dogs, brown and white
Four parrots, red, green and yellow
Three giraffes, yellow and brown
Two lions, gold and brown
And *one. . . guess what?*

Dominique McHugh (10)
Chetwynde School, Barrow-in-Furness

Santa's Sack

In his sack Santa hid . . .
Ten teddy bears, short, fluffy things
Nine bells going *ting*
Eight alarm clocks going *ring, ring, ring*
Seven musical instruments to make an excellent noise
Six sweets for all the good boys
Five music books so I can play whilst the others are eating
Four board games for the family
Three books, 200 pages each way
Two Xbox games, great to play
And *one . . . guess what?*

Christopher Belbin (9)
Chetwynde School, Barrow-in-Furness

The Tough Rhino

The tough rhino
A very angry creature
Tough, big, angry
Like a boulder with a horn
Like a train
It makes me feel weak
It makes me feel defenceless
The tough rhino
Reminds me of a dinosaur
That lived millions of years ago.

Howard Morgan (10)
Chetwynde School, Barrow-in-Furness

Pussy Willow

I have a favourite cat
Her name is Pussy Willow
And every night
When I'm in bed
She curls upon my pillow.

Jennifer Collings (10)
Chetwynde School, Barrow-in-Furness

The Mighty Tree

The mighty tree,
Its age can be found on its bark,
Huge, old, thick,
Like a skyscraper soaring above the clouds
Like a giant sand dune,
It makes me feel young,
Makes me feel like a newborn child,
The mighty tree
Reminds us how great nature is.

James Preston (10)
Chetwynde School, Barrow-in-Furness

Dogs

Wagging tails and digging paws,
Canine bed and doggy snores.

Barking for lunch, *munch, munch, munch,*
Meaty mouthfuls, *crunch, crunch, crunch.*

Playing fetch with a ball,
Dirty pawprints in the hall.

Doggy chews hats
And likes chasing cats.

Furry old doggy
That likes getting soggy.

Holly Hillman (10)
Chetwynde School, Barrow-in-Furness

The Tiny Ant

The tiny ant
So small you don't notice it
Tiny, weak, sneaky
Like a breadcrumb on the floor,
Like a spy sneaking around
It makes me feel like a huge giant
Like a huge monster everyone's scared of
The tiny ant
Shows us how tiny things can be.

Sam Storey (11)
Chetwynde School, Barrow-in-Furness

The Beautiful Stars

The beautiful stars
Billions of years old
Bright, beautiful, wonderful
Like torches being shone on Earth
Like shooting fireworks
It makes me feel dark
Like a candle with no flames
The beautiful stars
Remind us how far away we are.

Lorna Sharpe (10)
Chetwynde School, Barrow-in-Furness

The Roller Coaster

The roller coaster
Zooms at the speed of sound,
Strong, smooth, tall,
Like a snake swerving around,
Like a jet on rails,
It makes me feel like I'm flying,
Like a bird soaring through the sky,
The roller coaster
Reminds us of how fast we can go.

Theo Messenger-Jones (11)
Chetwynde School, Barrow-in-Furness

The Rushing Wind

The rushing wind
The everlasting blowing coming
Fast, strong, mighty
Like a car rushing through the city
Like a monster coming to get you
It makes me feel weak
Like a person as a train comes rushing past
The rushing wind
The power we do not have.

Ben Osborne (11)
Chetwynde School, Barrow-in-Furness

The Dark Cavern

The dark cavern,
Still here from the start of the Earth,
Dark, cold and deep,
Blunt daggers sticking out everywhere.
A dark portal leading to darkness.
It makes me feel tiny,
Like a speck of dust.
The dark cavern
Reminds us what we will destroy when we pollute.

Daniel Young (10)
Chetwynde School, Barrow-in-Furness

The Silver Moon

The silver moon
Is lit up by the sun,
Rocky, bright, misty,
Like a candle lighting up the sky,
Like a light you turn on and off,
It makes me feel cold,
It makes me feel like a moth looking up at a bright light,
The silver moon
Reminds me of how lucky we are to have light.

Anna Cooper (11)
Chetwynde School, Barrow-in-Furness

The Silver Moon

The silver moon
Up in space
Calm, round, relaxing
Like a 10p coin
Like a ball of tin foil
It makes me feel relaxed
Like not having anything to do
The silver moon
Reminds us that life keeps going.

Charlotte Smith (11)
Chetwynde School, Barrow-in-Furness

The Storm

The clouds are like leeches,
they suck the happiness out of the world.

The rain is like a rattlesnake
because of the rattling sound of the snake.

The wind is like a wolf
because it howls in the distance.

The thunder is like elephants
stampeding because of the booming it makes.

Amy Winskill (9)
Cinnamon Brow CE Primary School, Warrington

The Storm

The sleet is like a frisky horse jumping high and low.
The hail is like a giraffe eating leaves and grass.
The lightning is like a gigantic heavy whale
Splashing its tail on the water.
The thunder is like a demon, dark, cloudy and scary.

Emma McKean (8)
Cinnamon Brow CE Primary School, Warrington

The Storm

The dark is like a lion's wide open mouth,
Scaring all the night-time creatures.
The wind is like a werewolf, far away,
While the storm is heading towards us,
Like a herd of elephants!
Meanwhile, a dead body is in sight,
A cold, cold skeleton.

Jessica Hatton (8)
Cinnamon Brow CE Primary School, Warrington

The Storm

The storm is like a herd of elephants,
Stampeding in the mist.

The thunder is like a furious bear,
Growling for love.

The rain is like a horse,
Galloping for its life.

The wind is like a wolf,
Howling in the woods.

Alice Low (8)
Cinnamon Brow CE Primary School, Warrington

The Storm

The wind is like a werewolf howling at night.
The storm is like a stomp of an elephant.
The cold is like a frozen bone.
The thunder roars like a lion.

Lewis Hough (7)
Cinnamon Brow CE Primary School, Warrington

The Storm

The wind is like a motorbike thrashing all around,
The rain is like lava jumping out of a volcano.
The lightning is shining like thousands of electric eels.
The thunder is horrendous.
It sounds like horses racing
With all of the stamping of their hooves.

Shaun Hughes (8)
Cinnamon Brow CE Primary School, Warrington

The Storm

The storm is like a bull,
Raging towards a man in red.

The wind is like a tiger,
Running away from a hunter.

The thunder is like a lion,
Roaring fiercely.

The lightning is like a cat's eyes,
Glowing in the dark night.

Alex Cosgrove (8)
Cinnamon Brow CE Primary School, Warrington

The Storm

The lightning is like a cheetah that strikes at any time, strong and fast.
The wind is like a werewolf howling all night long, ferociously.
The rain is like a rabbit patting its feet, continuously.
The thunder is like a lion that keeps on roaring all the time.

Nicole Hodges (8)
Cinnamon Brow CE Primary School, Warrington

The Storm

The storm is like a lion roaring.
The ice and cold is like an ice demon
Casting a spell over the Earth.
The sky is like a family of black panthers galloping fast.
The wind is like an ape breathing heavily.

Ben Gough (8)
Cinnamon Brow CE Primary School, Warrington

The Storm

The thunder is like the furious roar of a lion
Hunting through the darkest Dementor in the world.
The storm is like a mammoth with great big gigantic feet,
Which makes the damp ground shake to the heavens.
The demon treasures its golden coins
And guards it till morning sun rises
And the dragon's fire is just like the strongest wind ever.

Eleanor Leach (9)
Cinnamon Brow CE Primary School, Warrington

The Storm

The wind is like a cheetah,
Speeding after his prey and then it catches it.

The dark is like a panther,
Jumping over the world.

The rain is like a leopard,
Light-footed and goes to hide its prey.

The lightning is like cats' eyes,
Glowing in the dark.

Louis Skinner (9)
Cinnamon Brow CE Primary School, Warrington

The Storm

The storm is like a fierce panda,
Stamping all over the place.
The lightning is like a snake,
Rattling its tail on its way.
Thunder is like a tiger roaring at everything,
The rain is like an amazing bird flapping its wings.

James Johnston (8)
Cinnamon Brow CE Primary School, Warrington

The Storm

The rain is like a slithering snake,
Hissing on the ground.

The thunder is like a savage werewolf,
Howling in the invisible air.

The wind is like a fierce lion,
Roaring in the midnight blues.

The dark is like a black puma,
Sleeping in a nearby tree.

Frankie Evans (9)
Cinnamon Brow CE Primary School, Warrington

The Storm

The storm is so dark it is like a Dementor
And its deadly black cloak.
The wind fiercely swoops down like a hawk.
The snow is like the Ice Age,
Only a mammoth could survive.
The lightning is striking so fast and furious
Like a cheetah.

Tom Meza (9)
Cinnamon Brow CE Primary School, Warrington

The Storm

The thunder sounded like a herd of elephants
Marching round the play area.
The coldness was like a hairless cat
Trying to stay out of the cold
And the darkness made it look like bats flying around.
The lightning was blinding,
It was almost like cats' eyes glowing in the dark.

Georgia Ratcliffe (8)
Cinnamon Brow CE Primary School, Warrington

The Storm

The thunder is like elephants
stampeding through the trees.

The lightning is like a zebra's
stripes flashing by.

The rain is like birds flapping
their wings furiously.

The dark is like bats sneaking
into the cave.

Meredith Wheeler (8)
Cinnamon Brow CE Primary School, Warrington

The Storm

The wind is like a giant werewolf,
Howling to the moon.

The lightning is like a striking snake,
Spitting venom at its prey.

The thunder is like a fierce lion,
Roaring as loud as anything.

The dark is like a black cat,
Attacking everything in its path.

Callum Halls (8)
Cinnamon Brow CE Primary School, Warrington

The Storm

The rain is like a big dragon roaring through the castle.
The clouds are like a lion sleeping or eating.
A cold forest is like a roar of a cheetah running wild.
The thunder is like a tiger eating and running wild.

Elizabeth Wakefield (9)
Cinnamon Brow CE Primary School, Warrington

The Storm

The storm is like a spotty cheetah
sprinting around the desert.

The lightning is like a scared bird
flapping its wings in big strokes.

The thunder is like a giant eagle
crashing down onto the floor.

The rain is like a greasy snake
spitting venom on metal.

Samuel Evans (8)
Cinnamon Brow CE Primary School, Warrington

The Storm

The storm is like a roar of the rainforest
Fiercest lion of them all.
The lightning is identical to the Great Fire of London
Burning everything that stands in its way.
The rain is like a gigantic flood in from sea
And a small tsunami.
The wind is like a wolf that howls out air
And overcomes gravity.

Kimberley Boot (9)
Cinnamon Brow CE Primary School, Warrington

The Storm

The storm and the rain was like an army of ants tapping by.
The thunder was like a T-rex stamping loudly.
The wind was like an owl calling and hooting for its teammate.
The lightning was like a grasshopper making its noise.

Adam Butler (8)
Cinnamon Brow CE Primary School, Warrington

The Storm

The thunder is like a starving bear,
Roaring for its food.

The wind is like an impatient werewolf,
Howling for freedom.

The lightning is like a fierce cheetah,
Striking to kill.

The rain is like an anxious rainforest,
Letting out its anger.

Georgia Everett (8)
Cinnamon Brow CE Primary School, Warrington

The Storm

The rain is like a fierce army of ants,
Searching for their destiny.

The sky is like a squid's ink,
Waiting to kill.

The lightning is like the chameleon's tongue
Thrashing through the sky, in and out.

The darkness is like sheets of black
And evil is poured all over the land!

Hannah Grant (9)
Cinnamon Brow CE Primary School, Warrington

The Storm

The lightning is like a snake striking in the air.
The wind is like cheetahs running fast into a wall.
The thunder is like an elephant stomping on the ground.
The storm is like smashing and crashing chains
Whacking on the ground.

Elliot McKenzie (8)
Cinnamon Brow CE Primary School, Warrington

The Storm

The wind is like a crying person
Gasping for air.

The rain is like a wet rainforest,
Full of water.

The cold is like 1,000 knives,
Stabbing people, making them so full of pain they feel frozen.

The lightning is like electric eels,
Making so much light, shocking anything in its path.

Kiera Gardner (9)
Cinnamon Brow CE Primary School, Warrington

The Storm

The rain is like a strong elephant
That goes stamping through the zoo.

The wind is like a furious lion
As it roars in the lake.

The lightning is like an angry buffalo
Running as it roars.

The dark is like a black panther
That hides in the cave.

Joshua Askey (8)
Cinnamon Brow CE Primary School, Warrington

The Storm

Cheetah, running round the racing track.
Storm, like a lion very fierce racing through the jungle.
Lightning, like a dragon's wings waving very strong.
Cold, like a train whizzing past the train station.

David Evans (9)
Cinnamon Brow CE Primary School, Warrington

The Storm

The thunder is like a stampede of elephants,
Crashing down the trees.

The dark is like a black panther,
Jumping over the earth.

The rain is like a dolphin's tail,
Splashing in the sea.

The cold is like a horse in winter
That doesn't have much fur.

Sophie Thomas (8)
Cinnamon Brow CE Primary School, Warrington

The Storm

The wind is like a dragon's wings
Chopping through the trees.
The dark is like the blackout,
There is no light all over the world.
The sky is like a lion roaring like a god.
The storm is like a knight, unstoppable.

Harry Judge (8)
Cinnamon Brow CE Primary School, Warrington

The Storm

The lightning is like a flash of fire,
Through the sky.
The thunder is like a stampede of elephants,
Stamping through the forest.
The rain is like a horse trotting,
Through the field.
The wind is like a bear roaring in the air.

Brittany Rachel Rose Fairhurst (8)
Cinnamon Brow CE Primary School, Warrington

The Storm

Thunder like a rattlesnake's tail rattling,
Wind like a dragon's wings flapping,
Hailstone like a horse's feet stamping on concrete,
Cloud like a cow's black and white patches.

Jessica Wall (9)
Cinnamon Brow CE Primary School, Warrington

Bump In The Night!

Aarrgghh! Who is it?
Aarrgghh! Who's there?
It's cold, I'm scared
Is someone there?
I've got a chill down my spine
Suddenly I hear a whine
My heart is beating fast
I hope this feeling does not last
The noise is coming closer and closer
Aarrgghh!
This is so traumatising
I hate it, I hate it
I am crying but no one can hear me,
'Mum, Dad, Mum, Dad, someone answer me please, please!'
I am shivering like mad
I wish this feeling would go away
Make it go away, make it go away!
It is real, I can't believe it
The walls are closing in on me
It was real, I was there . . .

Hannah Fell (9)
Corrie Primary School, Manchester

Fantasy Till Dawn

Walking down the beach, reins in my hand.
Heart beating like a drum, it's amazing.

Running into the water.
Splashing, falling.
Looking at his beauty.
He's irresistible.

Don't know what to do.
I feel his gaze upon me.
His soft skin against me
It's extraordinary.

It's late, I don't care.
The black figure still looks handsome.
It's magnificent.

I need to get home.
I'm getting scared.
It's going dark.
I need to get home.
I start running, running home.
He's following me.
I stop for breath.
I look at my watch.

I start running again.
I reach my house.
I don't see him.
He's gone . . .

With a flurry of his mane and the clicking of his hooves,
He's vanished out of my life forever.

Sarah Wilkinson (10)
Corrie Primary School, Manchester

Spook In The Night

Sitting on a hillside in a foggy mist
Curious, cold and forgotten
Lies an old creaking castle

Do ghosts lie within the haunted grounds?
Do skeletons stalk the haunted graveyards?

Inside the castle, armour moves
The spooky portraits with moving eyes
Follow you everywhere you go
Does anyone dare to go in there?

I stare up at the window
A glowing light flickers on
A withering face appears at the window
I gasp in shock
I don't know what to do
My heart is like a drum pounding and pounding
Help me, save me, save me forever.

Charlotte Law (9)
Corrie Primary School, Manchester

Winter Wondering

Irresistible frosty air around.
Please don't spoil the peaceful sound.
Frozen trees lie within.
Layers of ice are hard and thin.
Is that a person in front of me?
It's terribly foggy and I can't see.
The magnificent snow is cold and thick.
Frosty leaves you can't resist.
People make it look warm inside.
Couples sitting side by side.
Look at their faces as they glow.
Looking out into the immaculate snow.

Sarah Chadwick (9)
Corrie Primary School, Manchester

From My Window

From my window,
I can see a woman with flowers wilting in her hands.
I can see a chair as dark as the storm in the sky.
I can see a man with an army-green T-shirt
Like the trees prancing around in the wind.
I can see a cushion on the floor
With colours as light as the sunlit sky.

From my window,
The window is as grey as the smoke
Piling from a chimney top.
The rug on the wall is as high
As the whooshing colours in the rainbow.
The picture is as plain as the curtain with no patterns or colours.
The houses are small but big enough.

Danni Bersantie (9)
Darnhall Primary School, Winsford

Harpy Eagle

Sun is setting, moon is the only shining light,
Harpy's eyes open bright.
Wings spreading, calling proud,
Flying off to the midnight gown.
Streaking through the black dusk,
The silver lightning of darkness.
Swooping down, screeching loud,
Proving, he's the Olympian on wings.
Flying back to the cover of home,
Settling down, another night survived.
Shutting eyes, closing wings,
Just in time for the break of dawn.

Chloe Robinson (10)
Darnhall Primary School, Winsford

Death

He wanders the world all alone
With hair of fire and a head of bone.

You see his eyes, you know you're dead
You cannot hide under your bed.

A skeleton body with a cloak of black
He carries your soul away in a sack.

If you are old and it's the end of your day
He will come and take you away.

People curl and cringe in fear
Whenever the creature wanders near.

You cannot escape from the shadow of death
Wherever you are you'll feel his breath.

The terror is over: out came the light
But the monster known as Death will be out again
Tonight!

Simon Daniels (11)
Darnhall Primary School, Winsford

City Of Acroba

Walking through the shadows of night,
Where the moon sparkles in fright.
Children scared as they close their windows,
It switches night to dawn.
He runs away in the dark,
As the birds come out to play,
He stays in the dark and never comes out
Until night falls again in the City of Acroba.

Kristin Latham (10)
Darnhall Primary School, Winsford

The Crimson Killer

In the core of a forest,
A crimson and ivory coloured fox lurks here.
Seeking for fresh food to devour,
Mice scurrying as the crimson fox approaches.

The fox's ears prick
Like it's listening to something.

Claws as razor-sharp as knives,
Gleaming enough to see them in the darkness.
Its eyes glowing like two head lamps,
Shimmering in the shadowy night.

The crimson fox enters a farm,
He creeps into the hen house and . . .
Snap!

Jack Scott (10)
Darnhall Primary School, Winsford

Shark!

Swimming swiftly in the sea,
ripping you up with silence
but with unpleasant glee,
his pointing fin gliding,
across the deep blue sea,
fish go hiding,
so he doesn't find them,
he clobbers you as he smothers you,
biting away,
when you're fighting away,
so you can keep your life alive.

Christopher Bayliss (9)
Darnhall Primary School, Winsford

Death

As frozen as an Arctic glacier,
Just like hollow stones,
He stalks the misty graveyard,
His body rotting bones.

His face so lifeless,
Bony and dull,
No body, no soul,
No friends to have fun.

His fingers promontory like snapped twigs,
Elbows bony and pointy like a pin's end,
Fingernails as sharp as blades,
Cloak as black as the night sky,

You cannot stop Death.

Paul Hunt (11)
Darnhall Primary School, Winsford

Death In The Night!

Sneakily through the night,
He's out again, I catch a sight.

Stumbling the cobbles Death's bony body creeps,
Nobody notices, they're all asleep.

Eyes just like hard coal,
He hasn't even got a soul.

Everyone suddenly wakes up,
Death has gone.

Was it real or just your imagination?

Sarah Cooney (10)
Darnhall Primary School, Winsford

The Magic Box

(Inspired by 'Magic Box' by Kit Wright)

I will put in the box . . .
A strong man and a
stripe from a zebra,
A scale from a goldfish and a
spark from a burning flame.

My box is made of . . .
The poison of a viper,
burnt wood from a deadly flame,
teeth of deadly snakes.

I will put in my box . . .
A beam of light from the sun,
the blade of a pendulum
a trunk of a tree.

I will put in my desk . . .
A book with nothing on the pages.

Mark Latham (10)
Darnhall Primary School, Winsford

Death

The local undertaker that everyone knows,
Ghostly white like the forever lost souls.
He is as undetectable as God,
Collecting the deceased as his daily job.
Dishevelled like a pauper, he takes our souls,
His face so bony, his eyes like coal.
His crooked fingers are the key to every life,
His blood cold and his staring eyes like knives.
Feel his hands on your shoulder,
Feel his icy cold breath,
Beware, for his name is Death.

Ellen Bannister (11)
Darnhall Primary School, Winsford

The Wanderer

In the figure of a man,
Death walks the Earth.

His cold, empty voice,
Crying out in pain.

The graveyard silent,
He walks alone.

The headstones blurred,
By the ebony blanket that shadows the Earth.

Then in a split second,
The people of darkness emerge.

They capture the light,
The shadows disappear.

Total blackout,
Time has stopped.

It was all a dream,
It was not true, it was false.

Katie Bannister (11)
Darnhall Primary School, Winsford

Death

Death is black, death is white
He comes by day, he comes by night.

He'll come eventually, you can't hide
He even comes at Yuletide.

He moves like fog drifting over a graveyard
He moves like a dog sprinting on a farmyard.

He still lives on when all is gone
Death will get you one by one.

Luke Daniels (11)
Darnhall Primary School, Winsford

One Quiet Night

It was so quiet that I heard
An ant scampering across the lawn.
It was so quiet that I heard
A bag blowing along the street in the wind.
It was so quiet that I heard
A cat scratching at the fence.
It was so quiet that I heard
A woman brushing her hair in her bedroom.
It was so quiet that I heard
The trees tapping at the window.
It was so quiet that I heard
A man walking his dog.
It was so quiet that I heard
A leaf gliding down to the floor.
It was so quiet that I heard
An aeroplane flying in the distance.
It was so quiet that I heard
A shopkeeper locking up his shop.
It was so quiet that I heard
Raindrops pitter-pattering on the windowpane.
It was so quiet that I heard
The trees blowing in the wind.
It was so quiet that I heard
The binman emptying the bins early in the morning.

Mollie Bell (11)
Darnhall Primary School, Winsford

Death

In the starless night he stalks the Earth,
And drapes through the wind.
When you least expect it he strikes.
With a blade as sharp as claws.

His eyes are as crimson as fire that's burning hot,
Eyes like balls of blood that stare in the icy, distant night sky.

Gemma Clark (11)
Darnhall Primary School, Winsford

Death

Creeping in the cold night,
Death arrives to give you a fright.

Skeletal bone,
Eyes of empty, cold stone
His voice a deadly tone.

His lifeless body drifts around graveyards and homes.
Creeping round corners,
Listening like a predator awaiting its prey.

Death can destroy you,
Your friends too.
So *beware!*

When you get ill,
Death can kill
And make your blood spill.

So be careful when you sleep,
Make sure Death doesn't creep
And leave your body in a heap.

Asleep *forever,* awaking *never.*

Sophie Barker (11)
Darnhall Primary School, Winsford

Death Walks The Earth

People look, people stare,
Thinking, *is he really there?*

Looking near, looking far,
Whilst drinking ale at the bar!

A pale shadow rises up the walls,
Suddenly someone falls,

Death is there,
So be aware,

In the end Death will kill us all.

Lauren Clewes (11)
Darnhall Primary School, Winsford

The Artful Eyes

The dark black nose,
Like the dark black night,

The artful eyes in the glowing,
Face of the fox,

The ruby-red flames,
Like the remains of a fire,

The claws, as shiny like the
Silver, sharp knife,

The ears like a
Pointed quill,

The chestnut coloured fur,
On the soft, sly fox.

Katy Freeth & Sarah Koch (10)
Darnhall Primary School, Winsford

Death

Death is dark, Death is black
He hunts the Earth and drifts the night,

Death has a hood, he wears it on his head
To hide his bloody face away,

His bones are weak, his bones are bold
In a little hold they will break,

Death has a sword, it is as sharp as a cook's knife
His sword can kill in one stab,

His eyes are battered like boulders in the sea.

Jordan Humphreys (10) & Nicol Byrom (11)
Darnhall Primary School, Winsford

Death Star

Luke ignites his green lightsaber,
Then attacks the daunting Darth Vader.

The sabers clash together fast,
Like lightning striking with a blast.

Destroying planets with the Death Star,
Incoming fire coming from afar.

Luke trying to destroy the station,
Vader in a Sith Infiltrator.

AT-AT's attacking echo base,
All belong to an evil face.

Direct hit! There goes the Death Star
Loud cheers from Yavin 4.

Alex Taylor (11)
Darnhall Primary School, Winsford

Death - The Poem

As undetectable as holy,
Dressed in black rags, doing his daily job,
Torturing,
Bedraggled, begging tramp.
All mangled bodies damp in blood,
Coal stone eyes, as jet-black as a
Hidden underground cave,
Fingers crooked, all bones
Skeleton body
He'll take your soul
So watch out, Death is coming
To get your spirit!

Jessica Hardiman (10)
Darnhall Primary School, Winsford

Motocross

On the start line, ready to go
There's no time to see a rainbow

Out, out of the start gate along the straight
It's tough luck if you hit the start gate.

Around the first, you'd better watch out
If you break a bone you might go *ouch.*

Up the jump into the air
Argh! I saw a hare!

To the finish line now, it's the second lap
There's no time to have a nap

Cut the corner, you go zoom
You go faster than the moon.

Up the hill, get it in gear
Your dad's watching you, a rider's near.

Into the rut, you take the inside
You catch the rider by surprise.

Into second place now, keep up the pace
You might just win the race.

Over the tabletop, into the air
Come on! Come on! First place is there.

The final corner, only 00:01 seconds behind
Oh my God! you take the fellow by surprise.

A big gap now, the finish line's there
Yeah you've won, let's celebrate on the podium chair.

On the lap of honour is where you go
You're so happy and your family's stoked.

Conner Preston (10)
Darnhall Primary School, Winsford

Crowned At Birth

Chanticleer with golden orbs as eyes,
Which make him able to spot flies,
He can crow like no one else can crow,
Every time the ladies look at him he just takes the flow.

Everyone loves Chanticleer's lucky feather,
But most of all he's very clever,
Chanticleer's beak is like a shining star,
But Chanticleer is the best by far.

Chanticleer's crown is crimson flame,
But he's very vain,
His multicoloured chest is the best
Just like a bird in a nest.

Rowan O'Shea (11)
Darnhall Primary School, Winsford

Death

Skeleton as old as time,
Crooked fingers like the branches on a tree,
As undetectable as the Holy Spirit,
Dressed in black rags,
He goes around,
Killing,
Killing,
Like hollow stone,
As cold as ice,
He drifts the Earth,
All alone,
Alone.

Katherine Brittleton (11)
Darnhall Primary School, Winsford

The Magic Box

(Based on 'Magic Box' by Kit Wright)

I will put in my box . . .
the tooth of a blue shark,
the feather of a griffin
and the scale of a Nile crocodile.

I will put in my box . . .
the blades from an eagle's talons,
the charm of a dragon's flames,
the shine of a phoenix
and the jaws of a viper.

James Barratt (10)
Darnhall Primary School, Winsford

Death

Death drifts the Earth at nights alone,
He stalks the Earth at night,
His cloak is as black as the darkness,
He tricks you when you least expect it,
When you are alone Death will get you,
He never comes out in the daytime,
When he tenses his fingers they will crack.

Kelly Hutchins (11)
Darnhall Primary School, Winsford

Chanticleer

Feathers like the sunset.
Claws like daggers.
Beak as tough as a sword.
Tail as bright as the sun.
Crest like a blaze of fire.
Eyes as blue as the sky.

Samantha Hughes (10)
Darnhall Primary School, Winsford

The Cockerel That Was Crowned At Birth

Chanticleer can crow
like no other cockerel can crow,
every time the ladies look at him
he goes with the flow.
Chanticleer's crest is just the best,
but when he's with the ladies
he likes to take a rest.

Everyone loves Chanticleer's lucky feather,
but most of all he's very clever,
his beak is like a shining star,
but Chanticleer is the best cockerel by far.

Chanticleer's body is crimson flame,
but he also thinks he's very vain,
his multicoloured chest is like a vest,
just like a bird in a nest.

Jordan Fleming-Scott
Darnhall Primary School, Winsford

The Magic Box

(Based on 'Magic Box' by Kit Wright)

I will put in my box . . .
a fin of a fish,
a square tomato,
a hippo's tusk.

My box is made from . . .
ice from the North Pole,
lava from a volcano,
gold from a safe.

I will put in my box . . .
a ten-legged spider,
the north wind,
some magic dust.

Russell Heaton (10)
Darnhall Primary School, Winsford

Death

At the ring of one church bell
Death rises from his grave.

His face is as bony as a rusty shell,
His eyes, dark black you cannot be saved.

He approaches his prey and he pulls out his stick
And at the aim of one shot the prey is dead.

Is Death coming? Is he here? He's here taking his pick.
Watch out, here he comes, that eye drops a tear.

Where is Death, is he near?

His name is . . .
> Death!

Mark Robson (10)
Darnhall Primary School, Winsford

My Dad And Me

My dad and me do almost everything together,
No matter whatever the weather.
He takes me to football matches
And we cheer when Everton score,
It makes me want to go more and more.
I'll never forget him
And he'll never forget me.
We will always be there for each other
And share our problems, him and me.
But most important of all
We will always love each other for evermore.

Emma Hayes (11)
Darnhall Primary School, Winsford

The Canterbury Tales Poem

(Inspired by 'The Canterbury Tales' by Chaucer)

I saw a fox with a bushy tail,
I saw three rogues drinking ale.

I heard a cockerel pecking at the ground,
I heard that gold is what the three rogues had found.

I saw a cockerel escape a fox's jaws,
I saw the fox's shiny claws.

I heard a clanging funeral bell,
I heard that Death comes from Hell.

I saw the fox running for his life,
I saw the widow sharpening her knife.

I heard a cockerel crowing at the dawn,
I heard his seven hens in the lawn.

I saw Death run a blade through his heart,
I saw a hearse drawn by horse and cart.

I heard Death's old bones rattling,
I heard Chanticleer fly to a tree that was clattering.

I saw glowing eyes in my dream,
I saw the fox in a sunbeam.

Sophie Stockton (11)
Darnhall Primary School, Winsford

The Magic Box

(Based on 'Magic Box' by Kit Wright)

I will put in the box . . .
a ripped page of spells from a mystic spell book,
the swish of a silk sari on a summer night,
the sail of a seaworthy ship,
the smile of a newborn baby.

I will put in the box . . .
the flash of a spark rising from a telephone wire
the lunar craft from the first flight to the moon.

William Leslie Seward (10)
Darnhall Primary School, Winsford

The Fox

The sneaky, sly fox.
His teeth, like a sharp sword.
His eyes are like lightning bolts.
His ears, as sharp as blades of grass.
His fur is orange like the sunset.
His claws, like the blackest jet.

Adam Forbes (10)
Darnhall Primary School, Winsford

Memories

I remember when I went to Spain,
My baby brother was a moaning pain.
I remember when I did a modelling show,
We all went on stage looking like ice and snow.
I remember when I went to Disneyland,
Our hotel was very grand.
I remember when my nans and grandads died
It was so sad I cried and cried.
Memories good, memories bad,
Some memories make me mad.

Lois Light (11)
Darnhall Primary School, Winsford

The Cockerel

His claws are as sharp as blades,
His feathers of all different shades.

His voice, as sweet as a hummingbird,
The notes twist and turn like they're being stirred.

His scarlet crest is like a crown on his head,
His beak, as sharp as hardened lead.

Haleema Kara (11)
Darnhall Primary School, Winsford

Television Pictures

While we take our Coke and fries,
The TV tells of hate and lies,
Shows death beneath bright foreign skies,
Can you pass the salt?

Men with axes and saws come along,
And hunters sing their hunting song,
Animals will not be here for long,
Who's washing up tonight?

The icebergs melt and fill up the sea,
For the Earth is getting warmer that people can't see,
All life could die every last tree.
What ice cream have you bought?

Tanks appeared in a normal town on a terrible day,
But the inhabitants are not too sad to say,
That the UN came and chased them away.
Please sit down and eat your tea.

Although there are famine-struck people with no shoes,
There are kind people helping and taking away illegal booze,
So hopefully we will not have to watch sad things in the news,
Mum, this is boring can we watch something else?

Ben Murray (10)
Davenham CE Primary School, Northwich

What I Would Do

What would I do if I turned to you?
Where would you be? Would you turn to me?
I would say, 'Hi' to you, or should that be me?
Since that is the way it would probably be!
How many people would there be
When one turned to him and one turned to she?
That's what I'd do if you turned to me.
But if it will happen, we'll find out and see!

Rosy Deverall (11)
Davenham CE Primary School, Northwich

Darkness

I was alone in the dark,
But I wished I was in a sunny park.

The owls hooted
And with fright I was rooted!

The trees groaned and put out their claws.
They were about to grab me when I fell on all fours.

The wolves howled,
And I wished I was in a crowd.

What was that crack?
Something had fallen on my back.

Something flew towards me.
I wished I could see
What lay before me.

I felt a tail of a rat,
I wished I had my cat!

I woke up in bed,
I had banged my head!

Matthew Jones (11)
Davenham CE Primary School, Northwich

The Blitz

In the distance the sirens began
to wail,
In the panic I stood on my
cat's tail.
I ran to the shelter and
crouched down,
I heard the planes drone
over our town.
Down came the factories in the
dead of night,
It suddenly became a very
big fright.
As I smelt the smoke
I began to choke.
I got my gas mask and
put it on,
As I did the searchlights shone.

Bethany Wood (10)
Davenham CE Primary School, Northwich

The Wood Elf

Deep in the gloomy and mysterious forest lurked the wood elf.
Both capricious, yet majestic in appearance.
The nature-loving creature lowered her silk-soft wings,
Allowing a beautiful butterfly to land on her finger.
Her golden, curly locks tumbled past her tiny waist.
Her clothes were made from large leaves and her feet were bare.
Her feet scrunched up when the long feather ferns tickled her toes.

A branch cracked and the admirer was revealed!
The wood elf turned her head, and the resting butterfly retreated to
a calmer place.
The creature moved forward and being fond of dancing in
a circular manner,
She lured the admirer into dancing with her.
The admirer lost all track of time and was entranced.
The admirer's only hope of escaping from her spell was to see
past her looks.

Rowan Southern (10)
Davenham CE Primary School, Northwich

Anger

A raging group of dark, furious rhinos
A well in the middle of space
Thunder and lightning colours the dark gloomy sky
A 3 metre swimming pool full of blood.

Cody O'Pray (11)
Derwent Vale Primary School, Workington

Silence

A hot air balloon flying swiftly in the sky
Lavender wafting all around
Peace in the world
Crumbly candyfloss on the street
Sand, soft as snow.

Kerryn Milburn (9)
Derwent Vale Primary School, Workington

Love Is . . .

Marshmallows melting sweetly and slowly
Flowers opening like a new life beginning
Bold and beamish soft pink colours
Cupid flying over the bright blue sky
Birds chirping in the long distance
And melted chocolate is the taste of sweet love.

Jodie Armstrong (10)
Derwent Vale Primary School, Workington

Hate

Stale as disgusting cold blood
Hot blazing chillies
Crashing noisy thunder
Spreading scorching fire.

Callum Devlin (10)
Derwent Vale Primary School, Workington

Love

Smells like a poison made out of love.
It looks like fresh red roses.
It tastes like melting chocolate.
Sounds like birds tweeting.
Feels like a bath full of tulips.

Natalie Irving (10)
Derwent Vale Primary School, Workington

Sadness

A sorrowful undersized boy
A gloomy downcast dark room
A miserable still river
A grey hovering depression.

Cheyenne Blacklock (9)
Derwent Vale Primary School, Workington

The Strangest Feeling

A field of roses
A newly lit fire warming the coldest of hearts
A steaming hot bath filled with rose petals freshly picked
A heavenly choir singing a sweet melody, catching the hearts of many
A scent of a bouquet of flowers being left unnamed
                                    on a desolate doorstep.

Melanie-Rose West (10)
Derwent Vale Primary School, Workington

Love

Flowers waving in the summer breeze
They smell like freshly picked roses
Love is red, like flaming fire
Flames coming close to each other
Lovebirds whistling and singing in the trees
The sweet crunchy taste of sugar.

Simone Massey (10)
Derwent Vale Primary School, Workington

Love

Like a firework soaring through the night atmosphere
A chocolatey sugary sweet flavour
Reds and pinks everywhere
Roses in a summer estate
A silky soft cushiony feel.

Nicky Pattinson (11)
Derwent Vale Primary School, Workington

Love

A spurting crimson rose
Squashy cushion waiting to be hugged
Melted chocolate puddle
Birds chirping in trees
Roses dipping from the sky.

David Elliot (11)
Derwent Vale Primary School, Workington

A Wintry Poem

White sheets of snow, so silky and calm
Cover the forest floor.
Light from the sun, shining on the snow
Icicles hanging from the tree branches,
Snowflakes twirling like autumn leaves.
Ponds frozen like pieces of glass.

Sadie Page (10)
Duddon St Peter's CE Primary School, Tarporley

Jack Frost

Jack Frost, Jack Frost,
He's a cold old soul,
He lights up the lamps
With glistening snow,
At night you'll find him,
At day you might,
But you'd better watch out,
In case he gives you a *fright!*

Thomas Greaves (10)
Duddon St Peter's CE Primary School, Tarporley

A Winter Scene

Snow-covered trees, bare of leaves,
Branches reach out to grab you across the pale blue sky.
Icicles gleam, hanging on branches in the sunlight, slowly melting.
Plants fight the freezing cold, trying to grow up into the sunlight.
Snowflakes falling out of the sky like twirling ballet dancers.
Footprints knee-deep in the soft powdery snow.
Rough, bumpy, slippery in the sunlight, covered in a white blanket.
Sun shoots through the white-covered trees.
Will the snow stay?

Harry Tomkinson (9)
Duddon St Peter's CE Primary School, Tarporley

Snowy Winter's Day

The snow falling like pure white feathers from a swan.
Bright lights shine through the trees.
Ice crystals shine like diamonds.
Squirrels coming out to find their nuts.
Ducks on the ice, slipping and sliding,
Confused rabbits can't figure out where all the grass has gone.

Amy Hallam (11)
Duddon St Peter's CE Primary School, Tarporley

Snow And Ice

Snowflakes float from the sky
Like ballet dancers twisting down towards the earth.
Each snowflake has a unique pattern
Covering lifeless trees, fields and hills.
Jack Frost throws his icy spears, freezing ponds and lakes.
Drips of water form into crystal clear icicles.
Snowflakes still fall thick and fast.

Matthew Magee (11)
Duddon St Peter's CE Primary School, Tarporley

Winter Wonderland

It looked wonderful, magical even,
The winter sun burned through powdery snow-covered trees,
Sun made thick drifts shimmer like shiny crystals
Icicles sharp but beautiful and glittering
The breeze whistled through trees
As shrill as a high-pitched note played on a soft, silvery flute.
Squirrels scuttling across glittering frost hurrying home for warmth.
The woodland is a beautiful place.

Tom Okell (9)
Duddon St Peter's CE Primary School, Tarporley

A Winter Poem

Pure, thick, powdery snow,
Bright sun shining,
Icicles melting, disappearing slowly,
Footprints vanishing from the morning's warmth,
Narnia, turning into spring,
Frozen puddles starting to crack,
Snow falling gently off the trees,
Little streams flowing again.

Pippa Higgins (10)
Duddon St Peter's CE Primary School, Tarporley

A Winter Poem

Lifeless trees reaching out,
trying to grab you with their branches.
Crystal icicles reflecting back at you,
from the gleaming sunlight,
like a magical land,
with the sun shafting down.
Snowflakes drift to the ground,
settling from the dull grey sky.

Matthew Barge (10)
Duddon St Peter's CE Primary School, Tarporley

Winter Poem

Falling snow,
Clear blue sky,
Icicles shining like diamonds as the sunlight breaks through the trees,
The ripples in the stream sparkle,
Pawprints lie deep in the powdery snow,
The sun goes down,
Stars glimmer in the moonlight,
Trees sway in the wind,
The frost spreads,
Will Jack Frost catch you?

Rebecca Blagg (9)
Duddon St Peter's CE Primary School, Tarporley

A Winter Poem

Wind whistled loudly through the cold, bare trees,
Tall trees loomed over as if they were giant people,
Their ghost-like hands bearing down on the white wood,
Icicles hung from the branches of the sparkling white trees,
Snow slipped off the trees gracefully like angels landing on
                                        the powdery snow,
Sun gleamed through the branches like a headlight from a car.

Ben Leaman (11)
Duddon St Peter's CE Primary School, Tarporley

A Winter Poem

A frost-covered forest
twirling snowflakes tumbling down
icicles dangling off rough branches
sun breaking through the trees
owls hooting while foxes make deep tracks in the drifts
skates left by the pond
a winter wonderland for everyone.

Helena Grantham (9)
Duddon St Peter's CE Primary School, Tarporley

A Winter Poem

Snow, like glitter falling from the sky.
Bare trees reach to the night like ghostly hands,
The howling wind sails through the silence,
Icicles hang from trees like diamonds sparkling,
While ice puddles reflect the moonlight,
Trails of deep footsteps in the cold winter's night,
Magical, frosty leaves float elegantly, twisting and turning
like ballerinas,
The moon breaks through the trees making the snow glimmer,
The winter wonderland sparkles with snowflakes and ice.

Beatrice Benson (9)
Duddon St Peter's CE Primary School, Tarporley

A Winter Poem

Wind raced like a cheetah through the frozen night,
Snow drifted along in the rush of the wind,
Shimmering sunshine shone through the broken trees,
Dark blue skies began to turn light,
Wind rustled like howling wolves
Causing the trees to roughly sway.

Katie Blagg (10)
Duddon St Peter's CE Primary School, Tarporley

A Winter Poem

A blanket of snow falls from the sky
Covering the forest floor beneath
Thin layers of glazing ice over a crystal pond
Still, as the branches on the trees
Hard as a rock but calm as the seas
Snow tracks, deep and thick
Icicles dripping from the treetops, melting in the sun.

Kathryn Antrobus (11)
Duddon St Peter's CE Primary School, Tarporley

A Winter Poem

A harsh, sharp wind whistled through the snow-covered trees.
Through the bare, lifeless trees came a shooting sunlight.
Ghostly shadows assembled themselves on footprint snow.
Icicles draped from out-stretched branches
                                    looking like mischievous hands,
Waiting to grab you and take you away to their underground lair.
Hungry amber squirrels dug at frost-frozen ground hunting for nuts.
One glove, like a lost child was lonely draped over a bollard,
                                            waiting to be found.
Abandoned snowmen, limp and sad-looking,
                                melted in the afternoon sun.

Hannah Willcocks (11)
Duddon St Peter's CE Primary School, Tarporley

A Winter Poem

Snow falling like little white doves,
Trees layered with shimmering snow,
Honking geese glide down to the icy covered lake,
Waddling to find broken patches in the ice,
Dense snow-covered forest, vast and wide,
Ice sparkles like diamonds on the frozen lake,
Rabbits burrow to get out of the cold.

Oliver Deakin (10)
Duddon St Peter's CE Primary School, Tarporley

Wonderful Winter

Frost breaking through the midnight sky,
Moonlit magic lights the forest,
Snowflakes falling like diamonds, reflecting in the moonlight,
Wind whistling through the towering trees,
Shiny icicles hang from the treetops,
Animals seeking shelter, leaving behind their tiny tracks,
Slushy ice, melting to rain.

Holly Jenkins (9)
Duddon St Peter's CE Primary School, Tarporley

A Winter Poem

Snow falling like twinkling stars,
Frost falling from the sticky spider's web,
A white sheet of silky snow covers the forest floor,
Moonlight reflecting upon the crystal icicles,
The wind growling like an angry bear,
Birds singing softly in the high tips of trees,
Footprints laid on the forest landscape,
Winds sailing through the old, bare trees,
Snow skimming across the icy lake.

Joe Melody Rupnik (10)
Duddon St Peter's CE Primary School, Tarporley

A Winter Poem

Deep, thick, soft drifts of snow,
Sparkling in the sunlight,
Shining through the trees like crystals,
Jack Frost coming to get you,
Flakes falling gently onto the ground,
Like glitter falling from the sky,
Icicles hang on trees,
Trails of footsteps through the forest.

Abbie Mulherin (9)
Duddon St Peter's CE Primary School, Tarporley

Winter Poem

Snow gently fell to the ground like fluffy feathers,
Children had played in it, sledging and building snowmen,
Snow slipped off the trees gracefully like stars falling to the ground,
Icicles hung from the trees like a decoration on a Christmas tree,
The wind howled like a wolf as it sailed through the
                                    branches of the tall trees,
The tree's branches reached out like they were going to grab you
And take us to an underground world.

Tom Sarstedt (10)
Duddon St Peter's CE Primary School, Tarporley

A White Wonderland

Huskies charge, tracks appear
Whirling wind howling
Large swooping trees surround this place
Snow falling, falling.

White wonderland almost blue with cold
Sky, crystal clear
Little sun appears that day
Will it ever be right?

Shimmering, shining snowflakes fall
Like twinkling stars
The wind is strong and fierce
Flicking the trees back and forth.

Jade Derbyshire (11)
Duddon St Peter's CE Primary School, Tarporley

A Winter Poem

Moonlight shining bright,
A frosty, cold and peaceful night,
A thick layer of snow,
Small winds do blow,
It will be beautiful, come the morn.

Icy puddles, frozen hard,
Better than autumn's slippery mud,
Skate on the lake all night long,
It definitely would not feel wrong,
Such a beautiful winter's scene.

Elaine Mercer (11)
Duddon St Peter's CE Primary School, Tarporley

A Winter Poem

As the wind sailed through the trees,
Snow fell from the sky and gracefully landed
Like icing sugar dusting the cake.
Ice glimmered in the sunlight,
Winter birds glided through the air,
Trees blew and rocked from side to side,
Animals hibernated waiting for spring.

Jack Williamson (11)
Duddon St Peter's CE Primary School, Tarporley

My Home That's Far From Me

I wander from the window,
That I stay at when I'm bored,
I look out for my prince
And my home that's far from me.

The window brings in air,
When I try to sleep a tear drops,
One that's quite cold,
While thinking of my mother
And my home that's far from me.

A dragon of some type captured me,
One that's quite a mighty one,
That captured me,
I wonder if I'm ever going home,
My home that's far from me.

I miss my mother,
I cry a bit,
I want my home,
And I wonder if this will ever go,
The one thing I know, tomorrow's another day.

Molly Watts (10)
Fairfield Junior School, Widnes

Do You Know Where We Are Yet?

Today is the day that we play,
We run around and jump in the hay.

Do you know where we are yet?
If you don't here's a bit more.
My brother's rolling around on the floor,
Getting covered in horse manure.
Do you know where we are yet?

No, here's a bit more.
Clip-clop, clip-clop,
My brother turns round and runs for his life,
He runs into the tack shed.
My mum's cutting the bread with a knife.
The horse is walking, going into a trot,
Oh my God, how do you remember all this lot?
Do you know where we are yet?

Jade Corcoran (11)
Fairfield Junior School, Widnes

Life In Autumn

L eaves shatter in the breeze,
I n spring they love the breeze,
F orever life will be like this,
E nding with a silent hiss.

I n life it seems,
N ow is a different scheme.

A ll the different leaves start falling from different trees,
U nderground the rabbits get ready for the breeze.
T hey collect their nuts in a heap,
U nderground they are ready to sleep.
M usic comes from the birds that sing,
N ow wake up, it is time for spring.

Abbie Geraghty (11)
Fairfield Junior School, Widnes

Limericks

There was a young man from Turin
Who fancied a girl called Lynn,
They tested their fate
And went on a date,
But then the ceiling fell in.

There was a young man from Belize,
Who spoke Portuguese,
He caught the flu
So went to Peru
And there he continued to sneeze.

There was a young girl called Lynn
Who was incredibly thin,
She was so skinny
Poor young Lynny
Was blown all the way to Berlin.

Liam Sheeran (11)
Fairfield Junior School, Widnes

The Beach

As I make my way
Across the bay
Looking at the trees
Dancing in the breeze

I said to myself, 'My oh my'
As the stars flashed in my inward eye

As I was looking at the sea
I heard I had some company
It was my best friend Shannon
As we both lay upon the sandy bay.

Isabelle Smith (10)
Fairfield Junior School, Widnes

Mountain, Mountain

Mountain, mountain way up high
I can't find a way to climb.
When I am with you I can do no wrong,
So now I'll sing you my special song.
Mountain, mountain you are hard to reach,
The top of you is so hard to breach.
Your outer layer is so cold,
But inside you have a heart of gold.
You listen to my problems whenever I am down,
That is why I'm glad that you are around.
If you go I will be destroyed,
All my insides will lose their joy.
You are helpful in every way,
That is why I need you today.
There are people that don't like you,
I don't see why, you can help them solve their problems
Like you helped me solve mine.
Oh no! Now that you have gone
Your help and support to me
Our joy and laughter, has all gone.
Although you're unique
Your soul will always stay deep down inside of me.

Chelsea Wignall (11)
Fairfield Junior School, Widnes

Holidays

H ot summer days are the best
O n the sandy beach I lie
L ovely lilos floating in the sea
I ce cream melting in my hand
D ads that give you money for anything
A nd fairground rides that tip you upside down
Y ummy fish and chips as I walk down the beach
S wimming in the sea.

Alison Sparks (11)
Fairfield Junior School, Widnes

You Know!

I know the luckiest girl, you know
She gets everything she wants, you know
She really is quite spoilt, you know
Everybody loves her, you know
From her family, friends and even teachers, you know
She has money hidden everywhere, you know
In her pockets, purses and bags, you know
She has the loveliest long blonde hair, you know
And the loveliest bright blue eyes, you know
She has two houses with beds, you know
Two wardrobes, two tellies and videos, you know
She is incredibly talented, you know
She acts and dances and sings, you know
There isn't another girl quite like her, you know
Have you guessed who she is yet?
You must have, you know
It's me, Alyshea, of course you know.

Alyshea O'Neill (11)
Fairfield Junior School, Widnes

Bing Bing Bing Bing Bong

(Inspired by 'On The Ning Nang Nong' by Spike Milligan)

Bing bing bing bing bong,
as the birds sing their silly song,
they sing all day, they sing all night,
it gives the crocodiles a terrible fright.

Ping ping ping ping pong,
the crocodiles are very snappy,
they follow you while you're at the zoo
and don't look very happy.

Ding ding ding ding dong,
the elephants run a riot,
they stamp their feet right up the street
and can't be very quiet.

Jessica Wilson (10)
Fairfield Junior School, Widnes

The Living Sea

The sea whipped up silver spray in the moonlit night,
The waves crashed into the dam as if having a fight,
The scorching sun penetrated the dark,
All the fish fled from a mighty shark.
In the deep there was a whale,
Who got caught up in a shipwreck's sail.
And while it was down there in the deep,
It ate some fish and went to sleep.
The children played on a shipwreck,
While the stones and sand watched from the deck.
All the animals laughed and squealed,
There was a fish and even a seal.
Some fish are fat and some are thinner,
But most of them will end up as someone's dinner.

Thomas Dudley (10)
Fairfield Junior School, Widnes

Night And Day

On a cold, frosty night
With only the moon giving out light
A doll wakes up and comes alive
She jumps into Noddy's car and starts to drive
She takes out the blocks and starts to play
Until the morn and light of day

The clock strikes seven, time to awake
Where have these toys come from for goodness sake?
I'll put them away and start the day
It's time to go outside to play.

Chloe Jones (10)
Fairfield Junior School, Widnes

Holiday

Today is the day that we go on holiday
The dog barking, my sister squealing, 'Hip hip hooray'
My mum stressed
My dad moaning
This is going to be a hectic holiday

As the car wheels are spinning so is my mother's head
Me and my sister screaming
And the sweet harmony of my dad's voice shouting, 'Shut up!'

'Yes,' we all scream as we arrive at the beach
My sister rolling round in sand
My mum sunbathing in the sun
My dad eating ice cream
Me in the sea.

What a lovely holiday.

Kaylee O'Brien (11)
Fairfield Junior School, Widnes

Emerald-Green

Emerald-green is all I see
When I am with my special tree
When I look at his leaves
They're shining bright
Until one night
I could not see my special tree anymore
Me and my tree were history
Lonely me, lonely me
Where is my special tree?

Michael Matthews (10)
Fairfield Junior School, Widnes

Firework Night

The twirling light,
The coloured night,
Changes emotions from sad
To happy and glad.

The twirling light,
The coloured night,
The dull autumn sky
Filled with rockets that fly.

The twirling light,
The coloured night,
The banging noise that they make
Stirs the Earth with a shake.

The twirling light,
The coloured night,
I woke up, it would seem
It was only a dream.

Gareth Watson (10)
Fairfield Junior School, Widnes

Football Poem

The ball whizzed into the goal,
The crowd let out a roar,
England are the winners,
One-nil the final score.

All of the family came to watch,
But their special meal they could not touch,
The players were getting totally drenched,
But I don't suppose they cared too much!

Matthew McCormick (10)
Fairfield Junior School, Widnes

Poem

Flowers are pink
And roses wink,
Flowers are blue
And you are new.

A valentine bird flew by,
He said he could fly
And then he said goodbye
And I began to cry.

I drink a drink,
That made me think,
I went all pink
So I could think.

Hearts are red,
Flowers are new,
Honey is sweet
And so are you.

Abigail Turner (6)
Forest School, Timperley

Garden

I've got a butterfly collection,
They're very bright,
They give me a reaction,
In the middle of the night.

It's nearly Valentine's Day,
I'll give a card to the Queen,
She'll pay me,
With money that is green.

I have a dog,
Who bangs against the bed,
His name is Mog
And he always hits his head.

Connor Rutherford (6)
Forest School, Timperley

Hope

What colour is it?
Hope is a pink sheet of paper floating in the breeze.

What does it sound like?
It sounds like the toot of a whistle being blown.

What does it taste like?
It tastes of sweet honey on a piece of toast.

What does it smell like?
It smells like melted chocolate waiting on the table.

What does it look like?
It looks like a little butterfly fluttering in the sky.

What does it feel like?
It feels like relief that has finally happened.

What does it remind you of?
It reminds me of doves flying through the air.

Annabel Clark (10)
Forest School, Timperley

Fear

What does it feel like?
Fear feels like a thousand butterflies flickering through your stomach.

What does it sound like?
It sounds like a grey wolf howling full of anger and sadness.

What does it look like?
It looks like a lion ready to pounce.

What does it smell like?
Fear smells like fire expanding inside you.

What colour is it?
Its colour is a dark turquoise blackening out.

What does it remind me of?
Fear reminds me of a golden sword infected with poison dug deep
into my heart.

James Proctor (11)
Forest School, Timperley

Horror

What colour is it?
Horror is black like a doomed cave.

What does it sound like?
It sounds like blood dripping in the deepest dungeons.

What does it taste like?
It tastes like rotting souls on the edge of the forbidden graveyard.

What does it smell like?
It smells like the kitchen cellar of the long-forgotten castle.

What does it feel like?
It feels like a vampire piercing its teeth into my neck.

What does it remind you of?
It reminds me of the bloody footprints on my bedroom carpet.

Aishwarya Bhatkhande (11)
Forest School, Timperley

Hope

What colour is it?
Hope is a bright blue colour sparkling in the light.

What does it smell like?
Hope smells like a sweet-scented rose.

What does it taste like?
Hope tastes of a sponge cake that has just cooled down.

What does it sound like?
Hope sounds like a band of angels singing a sweet tune.

What does it look like?
Hope looks like a beautiful butterfly hovering round the garden.

What does it feel like?
Hope feels as soft and as light as a feather.

What does it remind you of?
Hope reminds me of home and my family.

Liberty Nicholls (10)
Forest School, Timperley

Darkness

What colour is it?
Darkness is as black as a raven circling in the sky.

What does it sound like?
It sounds like a steam train snorting and whistling.

What does it taste like?
It tastes like liquid rubber being rammed down your throat.

What does it smell like?
It smells like a burnt out fire, full of charcoal and evil.

What does it look like?
It looks like a jet-black tidal wave engulfing everything in its path.

What does it feel like?
It feels like a bitter cold wind stabbing into your throat.

What does it remind you of?
It reminds me of being in a small cramped cave without light.

Andrew Clucas (11)
Forest School, Timperley

Hope

What colour is it?
Hope is the colour of lilac flowers gently swaying in the wind.

What does it look like?
Hope looks like a butterfly fluttering in the summer sun.

What does it smell like?
Hope smells like a cool, fresh breeze out in the country.

What does it sound like?
Hope sounds like a chorus of angels singing in Heaven.

What does it taste like?
Hope tastes like butter melting into a slice of toast.

What does it feel like?
Hope feels like a soft silk dress swaying to and fro.

What does it remind you of?
Hope reminds me of happy bells ringing in the distance.

Alexandra Cupples (11)
Forest School, Timperley

Hope

What is its colour?
Hope is pink, the colour of the sky at sunset.

What does it sound like?
Its sound is like angels singing from above.

What does it taste like?
It tastes like tangy passion fruits exploding with juicy flavour.

What does it smell like?
It smells like toast with melted butter on top.

What does it look like?
It looks like a bright, shining star in the sky.

What does it feel like?
It feels like rain after a long drought.

What does it remind you of?
It reminds me of white doves spreading their wings.

Gabriella Seaton (10)
Forest School, Timperley

Fun

What colour is it?
Fun is a multicoloured rainbow.

What does it sound like?
Fun sounds like children laughing all day long.

What does it taste like?
Fun tastes like some fruit bursting with flavour.

What does it smell like?
Fun smells like hot dogs on a summer's day.

What does it look like?
Fun looks like a colourful carnival arriving in town.

What does it feel like?
Fun feels like leaping onto a bouncy castle.

What does it remind you of?
Fun reminds me of the last day of school, hooray!

Phillip Murphy (10)
Forest School, Timperley

Silence

What colour is it?
It is dark blue with a hint of black.

What does it sound like?
It sounds like a ghost twirling around a dark chamber.

What does it taste like?
It tastes like a barren desert.

What does it smell like?
Silence smells of a room full of people all silent.

What does it look like?
It looks like people who want to, but are unable to, speak,

What does it feel like?
Silence feels like being in an empty room.

What does it remind me of?
It reminds me of when you have to be silent but you don't want to be.

Jamil Latif (10)
Forest School, Timperley

Death

What colour is it?
Death is a deadly black, like an endless gloomy hole,
                                    plummeting into the unknown.

What does it smell like?
It smells of rotting carcasses long since forgotten.

What does it taste like?
Death tastes of sharp, fresh blood melting in your mouth.

What does it sound like?
It sound like the eerie calling of a vulture, swooping down
                                    to devour its prey.

What does it feel like?
Death feels like the slash of an icy cold steel knife ripping your skin.

What does it look like?
It looks like a murky river rippling menacingly in the shadows.

What does it remind you of?
Death reminds me of salty tears oozing out of despairing eyes.

Lucy Garratt (11)
Forest School, Timperley

Murder

What colour is it?
Murder is deadly black where there's no light, no happiness, nothing.

What does it taste like?
It tastes like lost souls wandering around Hell.

What does it sound like?
Murder sounds like daggers being sharpened.

What does it feel like?
Murder feels like a thousand knives being stabbed into your heart.

What does it look like?
It looks like death on a dark street.

What does it smell like?
It smells like bodies rotting in their graves.

What does it remind you of?
Murder reminds me of death and how black-hearted
                              some people can be.

Jessica Gaskell (11)
Forest School, Timperley

Love

What does love feel like?
Love feels like a tiny butterfly gliding around your body fluttering
faster and faster.

What does love sound like?
Love sounds like a million voices all singing together in harmony.

What does love smell like?
Love smells like a perfect red rose growing in a garden full of hope.

What colour is love?
Love is a rosy red colour, so bright it hurts your eyes.

What does love look like?
Love looks like a clear blue sky decorated with white doves
forming the shape of a heart.

What does love taste like?
Love tastes like a moist chocolate cake carefully covered in icing.

What does love remind you of?
Love reminds me of young angels peacefully sleeping
in beds of feathers.

Sarah Nicholson (11)
Forest School, Timperley

The Colour Of A Rainbow

Happy as a bright yellow sun glowing hotly.
Nervous as brown mud which my mum puts in my shoes.
Angry as a drum being banged on the table.
Great is a gold wall shining in the sun.
Upset is a purple hat a clown wears.
Sad is a grey elephant sitting on a couch.
Scared as a blue cloud that is being covered by a rain cloud.

Bradley Stephenson (8)
Glazebury CE Primary School, Glazebury

Feelings And Colours

Petrified is as brown as a frozen statue.
Angry is as black as a cave hidden in the distance.
Sad is as grey as a cloud on its own.
Nervous is the silence of a school assembly.
Hyperactive is as multicoloured as a rainbow.
Happy is as light brown as a loving dog.
Excited is as yellow as a balloon.
Great is as red as a glowing sun.
Thoughtful is as orange as a helpful and nice lion.
Embarrassed is as dark blue as a kid dropping his pants in class.
Grumpy is as purple as a car being left in a dump.

Ellis Carney (8)
Glazebury CE Primary School, Glazebury

What Do I Feel?

As curious as a yellow sun shining in the summer.
As petrified and as blue as an icicle about to smash.
As embarrassed as a face turning purple.
As excited as a scarlet firework about to make a bang.
As happy as an orange pumpkin at Hallowe'en.
As delighted as a lilac sleeping bag at my sleepover.
As lonely as an empty suitcase locked in the loft.
As bored as a white snowman when his builders have gone for tea.

Abbie Lynch (9)
Glazebury CE Primary School, Glazebury

Rainbow Colours

Rainbow colours are so nice,
I think they are so beautiful,
Here they are . . .

Joyful is as multicoloured as a scarf on a windy day.
Scared is a dark green swamp on a dull day.
Happy is as yellow as the classroom walls on a sunny day.
Angry is as dark as a mean devil.
Sad is as orange as a small orange fish in the sea.
Upset is a brown tree bark on a rainy day.
Embarrassed is as light blue as the sky.
Nervous is as grey as a school playground.
Anxious is a light green colour like geography books.
Grumpy is as black as a dull night sky.

Thomas Chadwick (8)
Glazebury CE Primary School, Glazebury

Feelings And Colours

Happy is as blue as an elephant rolling in some mud.
Sad is as grey as a cloudy day when you can't play.
Upset is as black as a midnight sky being hated by a boy who wants
to go out and play.
Bored is as brown as an untuned violin.
Grumpy is as red as an apple being eaten when it doesn't want to be.
Gloomy is as dark blue as a cold, miserable dictionary not being used.
Hyperactive is as multicoloured as a rainbow.
Embarrassed is as light brown as a belt being dropped in class.
Delighted is as blue as wrapping paper being thrown on the floor.
Excited as a roar when Man U score.

Nathaniel Pestell-Jones (8)
Glazebury CE Primary School, Glazebury

Different Feelings

Excited as a boy when he gets an orange book of rhymes.
Hyperactive as a girl seeing a multicoloured rainbow for the very
first time.
Bored as a brown dog when the owners don't play with him.
Gloomy as a girl when the grey cloud comes out and covers the sun.
Embarrassed as a boy when his trunks fall down at the swimming pool.
Miserable as a boy when his mum gets him a dark green jumper.
Lonely as a girl when there's no one to play with.
Delighted as a group of people when the sun comes out.
Petrified as a girl screaming when somebody jumps out at her on
a dark, stormy night.
Grumpy as a man when no one visits him in a care home.

Lucy Johnson (8)
Glazebury CE Primary School, Glazebury

The Days Of Rhyme

Great is as yellow as some cheese going into a pizza.
Excited is as green as a caterpillar turning into a butterfly.
Hyperactive is as loud as children playing tig.
Happy is a pink flower opening up.
Terrified is as brown as a bear walking into a dark wood.
Miserable is as grey as an elephant charging towards me.
Nervous is as silent as someone embarrassed.
Delighted is a yellow bright sun in the sky.
Graceful is as pink as a ballerina on the stage.

Grace Hindley (8)
Glazebury CE Primary School, Glazebury

Horrible Days/Wonderful Days

Miserable is as black as a cave, in there on your own.
Joyful is as pink as a flower which smells like loads and loads
of sweets.
Anxious is as silver as ice skating, having never done it before.
Embarrassed is as brown as being drunk and kissing your enemy
in front of everyone.
Petrified is as dark as an orange not seeing your girlfriend on your
second date.
Bored is as grey as a rotten pear being sick all day.
Delighted is a light yellow, being a baby duck so cute.
Gloomy is a dark green like an ogre's face being sick on you.
Hyperactive is as multicoloured as a parrot pooing on your face.
Graceful is light blue like being in the sky and throwing up on a plane
at night.

Todd Edgar (8)
Glazebury CE Primary School, Glazebury

Untitled

As happy as Rio when he scored his goal.
Silent as the PlayStation when it's not being used.
As yellow as the sun on a summer's day.
As pink as my mum's coat when she walks my dog.
As white as a polar bear on a winter's day.
As bright as my dog's coat when it is on a walk.
As sad as a lonely elephant in the jungle.
As miserable as a black cloudy day.
As delighted as a frame on the wall on a sunny day.

Harry Spencer (9)
Glazebury CE Primary School, Glazebury

Untitled

Happy is as green as the sun making more light.
Great is as orange as a flower on the beach.
Sad is as blue as the rain in the sky.
Excited is multicoloured like a rainbow in the sky.
Grumpy is as grey as the sky on a rainy day.
Lovely is as red as the houses on a street in the summer.
Furious is as black as a man in the rain.
Delighted is as yellow as a sunflower in the sun.
Unhappy is like a baby crying because it is stuck in a box.
Petrified is like a man screaming up a tree.

Joe Love (9)
Glazebury CE Primary School, Glazebury

The Good Days/Bad Days

Delighted as a yellow classroom table.
Frightened as a purple hippopotamus being poked with a stick.
Joyful as a big juicy red apple.
Gloomy as a mixed grey and white horrible rainy day
                                        and you can't play out.
Excited as going round a multicoloured planet.
Miserable as dark green, soggy, wet grass,
As happy as a creamy brown Labrador puppy.
Anxious as a grey miserable day.
Graceful as a happy, blue, calm sea.
Bored as a black leaf that is dead on the floor.

Morgan Fearnley (9)
Glazebury CE Primary School, Glazebury

Untitled

Happy is as yellow as the bright sun.
Sad is as black as the sky at night.
Angry is as red as a man that's been hit.
Scared is as blue as the sea.
Bored is as green as the trees.
Gloomy is as brown as wet wood.
Nervous is as white as the white board.
Glad is as pink as a girl's cheek.
Grumpy is as grey as a cloudy sky.
Lonely is as orange as the sun coming up.

Harry Love (8)
Glazebury CE Primary School, Glazebury

I Had A Dream

I had a dream.
It was about a manor.
The sound of pattering feet.
The wind blowing outside the manor.
The cries and yells of servants.
It broke my heart to think that people were treated as badly as this.
The clinks and clonks of swords, and the raindrops on the roof,
There was something wrong.
I knew it was strange.
I couldn't wake up.

I was like lead,
I was nailed,
I could not move,
I was trapped . . .
Tortured
Encased
Entombed . . . but it was only the sheets around my legs.

Jennie Richmond (9)
Golborne Community Primary School, Golborne

Sea Dream

I go to bed to have a dream.
Go to sleep and dream of the sea.
Dance with the jellyfish
Swim with the sharks
Blow with the fish,
Jump up with the dolphins,
Eat fish with killer whale,
Slither with the electric eel,
Glance at the boats,
Catch fish with the fisherman,
Steer the wheel with the driver,
Rescue with the lifeguard,
Dive in the water with the mermaids,
I wake up after my dream,
Refreshed, invigorated, full of steam.

Lizzie Pilling (8)
Golborne Community Primary School, Golborne

My Dream

I had a dream that I was a rabbit with long, floppy, grey ears.
I hopped upon the hills and drank the water from the river.
My short, white, fluffy tail wiggled as I hopped.
I had a friend rabbit with me and we both hopped together,
And we both drank the water from the river.

The dream went on over the hills and far away . . hippity . . . hoppity . . .
far away . . .
my rabbit friend and I
                    We both hopped
                    We both stopped
                    We both gasped
                    We both stared
My rabbit friend and I.

Bethany Wilding (8)
Golborne Community Primary School, Golborne

My Dream

In my dream, my dream, my dream, I was a tiny mouse.
In my dream, my dream, my dream, I lived in a tiny house
with sweet green grass and delicious corn.
I fell off a cliff.
It turned out the cliff was my bed
and when I came down I had a big bump on my head.
The next night I went to bed with a big bump on my head.
I stayed awake all night thinking about my dream
and I knew it would continue.

My dream . . . in my dream . . . dream . . . dream . . .
My dream . . . in my dream . . . dream . . . dream . . .
Come true my dream,
My mouse,
My tiny house with sweet green grass and delicious corn
. . . bring true the memories of the life of dreams.

Charlotte Govan (7)
Golborne Community Primary School, Golborne

My Dream

My dream would be to be a millionaire and own my own furry mirrors,
with lots of animals and have a garden as big as two schools,
with flowers that never die.
To have a door in one of the trees in my garden,
and through this door there would be a new land of *chocolate*
that never goes out of date.
With ice cream falling out of the sky instead of rain.
Houses made out of candy with a pool as big as a school,
a rainbow you could walk over,
where the sun would be made out of money
and there would only be *me* who knew about it.

Nicole Thompson (8)
Golborne Community Primary School, Golborne

Dreams

Last night when I was in bed, many thoughts zoomed in my head.
Like buzzing bees and chocolate trees.
One seemed to slither out of my head, it was a bad one, a scary one.
It was about buzzing, stinging bees and scary chocolate trees.
I was so glad that it went!
Dreams can be good.
Dreams can be bad.
Dreams can be cool.
This one made me a fool.

Helen Taylor (8)
Golborne Community Primary School, Golborne

A Winter Poem

A winter morning
Nice and cold,
Waving trees
Stand out bold,
Cloudy skies
Dull and white,
Shivering people
Having a snowball fight.

Tall trees
Brown and rough,
Feel the air hit me
Hard and tough,
The tree's hands are cold
His bark overcoat keeps him warm,
While snow slides smoothly
And the sun shivers calm.

Lewis Harry (10)
Halton Lodge Primary School, Runcorn

Winter

Following me,
Silently, slowly following me
Your icy cold breath
Freezes me
You ensnare me in your fortress of ice
I can't break free from your dreadful grasp.

But soon your power will be shattered,
Your kingdom will be no more,
For spring will beat you like a battle won in a war.
You will no longer sit on your snowbound throne
And we will not hear your whistling moan,
Well not for another year that is!

Emma Sheakey (11)
Halton Lodge Primary School, Runcorn

The Future

In the future I'll be taller
In the future you'll be smaller.

In the future I'll be faster
In the future you'll be slower.

In the future I'll be wiser
In the future you'll be like a tiger.

In the future I'll be bolder
In the future you'll be older.

In the future I'll be mayor
In the future you'll be greyer.

But overall I'll still be me
And you'll always be you!

Natasha Wightman (10)
Heversham St Peter's CE Primary School, Milnthorpe

The Image Collector

(Inspired by 'The Sound Collector' by Roger McGough)

A strange man called this morning
Dressed all in black and white
He put every image in a sack
Then disappeared out of sight

The light out of the fire
The image of the bath
The hands of the grandfather clock
It made me start to laugh

The toast from the toaster
The tea from the pot
The glasses from the cupboard
It sounds like rather a lot

A strange man called this morning
Dressed all in black and white
He put every image in a sack
Then disappeared out of sight.

Maria Inman (11)
Heversham St Peter's CE Primary School, Milnthorpe

Blacksmith

Blacksmith
Hammering
Black shiny metal
Blacksmith
Beating
Shape out of iron
Blacksmith
Banging
In the heat of the fire
Blacksmith
Curving horseshoes.

Phillip Armstrong (8)
Heversham St Peter's CE Primary School, Milnthorpe

Beach Fever

I must go down to the beach again
To see the kiddies play
Watch them lick their ice creams
Until the sky turns grey

I must go down to the beach again
And watch the time fly by
Painting boats and gulls all day
Till the sun dies from the sky

I must go down to the beach again
To walk the sandy lawn
And show my friend dolphin
The pictures that I've drawn

I must go down to the beach again
To hear the seagulls search
To see the dolphins jumping
And adore the crowded beach.

Georgia Nield (10)
Heversham St Peter's CE Primary School, Milnthorpe

Sea Poem

I must go down to the sea again,
To see the washing waves;
Away from all the city smoke and
To the man in the deckchair that bathes.

I must go down to the sea again,
To see the seagull's nest.
I sat for hours and hours one day,
While eating an orange zest.

I must go down to the sea again
To play in the wet and soft sand;
With my bucket and spade and happy smile,
When the sand gets stuck in my hand.

Katherine Atkinson (11)
Heversham St Peter's CE Primary School, Milnthorpe

Let Them Wear Purple

When I am an old woman,
I will wear purple all the time,
I'll have a stick,
And rattle the railings with it.
Maybe I'll pretend people are railings.
I'll be purposely slow
To . . . cross . . . the . . . road,
They won't beep their horns at me.
After all, I'm just a poor old dear,
Crossing the road.
Hee, hee, hee.
I'll shout at all those really stupid people.
They won't call me impolite,
I'm obviously old and need care.
I'll buy a parrot
And train it to repeat every word I say.
Just to wind people up.
But I'm not an old woman yet.
I've got a long way to go until then.
But maybe doing all this at once will be difficult,
I think I might start to practise,
After all,
Let them wear purple.

Alice Pickthall (11)
Heversham St Peter's CE Primary School, Milnthorpe

Gold

Gold is a sunshine twinkling brightly in the sky,
Gold is money rattling in my pocket,
Gold is a ring shining on my finger,
Gold is a bracelet gleaming in my dark drawer,
Gold is a crown on my golden hair
Sitting on the throne;
Finally,
Gold is a sunset, blazing goodnight.

Megan Carling (9)
Heversham St Peter's CE Primary School, Milnthorpe

The Future

If you once found a time machine
What would you do?
Well I would jump inside,
Is that the same for you?

To find the mysteries of the new and the old,
Come inside, but it's not to be told.
Let's see the robot's computer head,
Are they made of metal or maybe lead?

People are in fast flying cars,
It takes seconds to get to Mars.
But what does the future hold?
Amazing things we are told.

So just wait here for a few more years,
Until the future reappears.
All of these might come true,
Maybe robots could replace you!

Jessica Pickthall (10)
Heversham St Peter's CE Primary School, Milnthorpe

My Nan

My nan might be getting old,
But she is a very special lady.
She has a kind and gentle face
Always smiling very cheerfully.
It looks so creased and wrinkled
Just like a silvery spider's web.
Her pale blue eyes deep like the ocean
Flitting everywhere, seeing everything.
Her tiny, crinkly crimson lips
Stretch and smile like an elastic band.
Small crumpled hands sit on her lap.
With long turquoise veins like flowing rivers.
My nan might be getting old,
But she is a very special lady.

Charlotte Thwaites-Breed (10)
Heversham St Peter's CE Primary School, Milnthorpe

My Mum

My mum has a very kind face
But sometimes it's cross and stern.
When I look into her eyes
They twinkle back at me.

She has a friendly voice
And her ears are always alert.
Her hands are long and slender
And they make me feel safe.

When she walks, she walks quite fast
And when she sits she is elegant.
I like the way she wears her clothes
She makes me very proud.

I love my mum and she loves me.

Joanna Peers (10)
Heversham St Peter's CE Primary School, Milnthorpe

The Future

In the future we might be able to fly to the moon,
A baby might be born in a balloon.
In the future my hair will be grey,
People might even eat hay.
In the future animals might be blue,
Paper might be made with glue.
In the future I will be older,
I certainly will be bolder.
In the future I might be greyer,
I might even be a football player.

Zak Crosby-McCann (9)
Heversham St Peter's CE Primary School, Milnthorpe

Scared

I am scared of people
Jumping out on me,
Loud banging noises
Startling me.

I am really scared when
Waking in the night,
There are lots of creaking noises
With no one else in sight.

I am really, really scared of spiders
Because when I go to bed
They are on the ceiling above me
About to drop on my head!

Francesca Ely (8)
Heversham St Peter's CE Primary School, Milnthorpe

The Future

In the future I might invent a time machine,
Or I might be a millionaire or even a billionaire.
My friends might be prime ministers,
Or they might be gangsters with guns.
My job might be a touring car driver
Or it might be nothing exciting.
My car might be a Ford Mustang Cobra,
Or it might be an old Beetle.
I might live in a huge old mansion,
Or I might live in a tatty scrapyard.
In the future anything could happen to me!

Alex Child (9)
Heversham St Peter's CE Primary School, Milnthorpe

The Life And Times Of Me And My Zimmer Frame

When I grow old,
I'll shake my Zimmer frame
at those young buffoons.
I'll have a big purple cloak,
just to be different.
I'll probably have a couple of walking sticks
and be incredibly slow getting on the bus.
But because I'm just a poor little old lady,
they can't tell me to get on with it.
Ya boo sucks to them!
I'll get a giraffe and keep it in the garage.
I think I might constantly disagree with people,
just to wind them up.
I will tell ignorant, fidgety little children,
that they have ants in their pants.
But because I'm old,
they'll just think I'm mad
and should be in a home.
Yes, I'll do that, and a bit more,
but right now,
as I'm still only a beautiful little darling,
I think I'll concentrate on the big purple cloak bit.

Eilish Halford (11)
Heversham St Peter's CE Primary School, Milnthorpe

Black

Blacksmith smashing, sparks flying everywhere.
Black beetles scuttling across the stone floor.
Black scorpion threatening with its tail.
Black slug sliding slowly slimily.
Black gorilla beating his chest in anger.
Black charcoal burning.
Black bat swooping,
Twirling in the black night.

Ritchie Budd (8)
Heversham St Peter's CE Primary School, Milnthorpe

Black

My dad's hair
My pumps
Metal chair legs
Black pen
Black sheep
Evil and naughty
Wizards and witches
Black is the colour of their cauldron for magic potions
Flies and bees and bullet ants crawling around
Stereo speakers
Thumping noise
black places
Like caves and haunted houses
Black is a colour
That makes you scared
Night-time is dark
Alone in my room
I keep a light on
To brighten the gloom.

Elliot Handley (7)
Heversham St Peter's CE Primary School, Milnthorpe

Black

A black scary book,
Horrifying black bear,
My really stinky pumps,
A black batty pen,
Big hairy spiders,
Crawling over me!
Scaly snakes trying to scare
You and me.
Do you know what?
It slid through a tree!

Heather Wilkins (7)
Heversham St Peter's CE Primary School, Milnthorpe

The Shape Collector

(Inspired by 'The Sound Collector' by Roger McGough)

A stranger called this morning,
Dressed in yellow and red,
Put all our shapes into a bag
And took them home to bed.

He took the circle from the saucepan,
The circle off the clock,
The circle on the bedpost
And the circle on our brand new lock.

The rectangle of the rubber,
Rectangles from the books,
The rectangle from the doorway,
Of the man that gives you nasty looks.

The squares in the window,
The squares off Mum's best plates,
The squares off the blackboard
And the squares on the sea where everyone waits.

A stranger called this morning,
He didn't leave his name,
Left us only squiggles,
Isn't that a shame?

Sophie Richards (9)
Heversham St Peter's CE Primary School, Milnthorpe

The Chocolate Man

Mother, while you were at the cookery class,
I was reading in my chair.
Suddenly at the window,
A huge great chocolate man was there.

He looked so tired and sleepy,
I decided to invite him in.
I even made him a cuppa,
While his dog jumped in the bin.

He stood in front of the fire,
In a weary exhausted pose.
He flopped in Dad's best chair
And had a little doze.

I sat there watching him,
Counting woolly sheep.
I must have got so tired,
I had a little sleep.

I suddenly awoke,
To find him not there.
I had no idea,
Exactly . . . where!

(Oh and by the way his puppy did a doo-doo on the floor!)

Holly Robinson (11)
Heversham St Peter's CE Primary School, Milnthorpe

The Colour Collector

(Inspired by 'The Sound Collector' by Roger McGough)

A stranger called this morning,
Dressed in bright pink foam,
Put all the colours in a bag
And carried them to her home.

She took the colour from the sun
And the blue from the sky,
The purple off my jumper
And the black from a swatted fly.

She took the green from the grass
And the white from the cloud,
The gold from the trumpet,
That wasn't very loud.

A stranger called this morning,
Never left her name,
I don't know what I'm going to do,
It will never be the same.

Rosanna Ely (10)
Heversham St Peter's CE Primary School, Milnthorpe

What Is The Moon?

The moon is a pot of ink
Splatting itself all over a piece of paper.

The moon is a yellow duck
Swimming in a muddy swamp.

The moon is a strike of lightning
Hitting a dark brown tree.

The moon is a dancing daffodil
Prancing round the flowerbed.

The moon is its shimmering self
Floating in the dark misty sky.

Rachel Nield (8)
Heversham St Peter's CE Primary School, Milnthorpe

White

White snow is cold,
a sparkling bright colour.
Polar bears camouflage
in their background of snow.
White is the skeleton
bones in your body.
Soft cotton wool balls
that rub nail polish off.
fluffy white clouds
sail across the sky.

Sophie Watson (7)
Heversham St Peter's CE Primary School, Milnthorpe

Blue

Blue as the sky
On a hot perfect day.
Blue as the sea
Making waves
And moving pebbles
Onto a sandy shore.
Blue as the clean smooth lake
With reflections of trees.
Blue as the refreshing rain
Dropping on the windowpane.

George Pickthall (8)
Heversham St Peter's CE Primary School, Milnthorpe

Black

Black is the colour of the night sky.
Black is the colour of my stereo.
Black is the colour of my cat.
Black is the colour of my dad's car.
Black is the colour of my pumps.

Benedict Willacy (8)
Heversham St Peter's CE Primary School, Milnthorpe

The Sea

The sea is a king cobra,
Strangling boats to munch;
Looking for people to gobble
Slithering around its lunch.

    The sea is a king cobra,
    Hissing at the boats,
    Moving slowly across the sea
    Gliding like a long float.

The sea is a king cobra
Pouncing on its prey,
Curling around the boats
Breaking them in half every day.

    When the king cobra is tired
    The sea is calm and still
    The king cobra sleeps quietly,
    Having now eaten its fill.

Ed McGaulley (7) & Sam Coates (8)
Heversham St Peter's CE Primary School, Milnthorpe

Red

Red is for roses
Red for dancing shoes
Red for a ruby
Too precious to lose.

Red for a woolly jumper
Red for your glossy lips
Red for a pretty skirt
Which is too tight at the hips.

Red for beautiful sunset
Red for a recycling box
Red for danger
And sometimes red is for a fox.

Megan Byles (8)
Heversham St Peter's CE Primary School, Milnthorpe

Blue

Sea is swaying waves side by side.

Blue is paint that is messy,
I wonder what else it could be?

Blue paper rips, strips by strip.

Blue trays are blue and still.

Pencil cases can be blue,
You buy them from the shops.

Crayons that colour in stuff
You need blue.

Jumpers you can use for winter
When you go to school.

Blue carpet you stand on,
It makes blue come up your hand.

Blue are the stars twinkling in your eyes.
Blue is the colour of my poem.

Tara McGaulley (9)
Heversham St Peter's CE Primary School, Milnthorpe

Green

Green is . . .
Grass sparkling in the morning dew.
Leaves blowing in the wind,
Sometimes falling like a raindrop from the sky.
Paint blobs on my paper, fresh and new.
Broccoli and cabbage in a rabbit's mouth.
Slime in a snail trail all green and yuck.
Lime, a slice on my cup, trickling in my Coke.
A crayon colouring the green, green grass on the hills.
Green is
All around us!

Dominique Davies (8)
Heversham St Peter's CE Primary School, Milnthorpe

The Awful Day

In the window you can see
The frosty fields immediately
With the glistening icy and crunchy snow
You can hear the whistling wind blow
Believe me, with all that ice
When I went out to play it wasn't nice!
My cold toes began to freeze
Leaves were rustling in the trees
Then suddenly it began to rain
The door opened and the teacher came,
'Time to come in,' the teacher said
As rain came dripping on my head
I went in and sat down
There were footprints on the ground
Well I have to say;
'It's definitely . . . an awful day!'

Holly Watson (9)
Heversham St Peter's CE Primary School, Milnthorpe

My Dog Sophie

My dog Sophie is a friend to me,
I've had her since I was three.
She comes to school almost every day,
She loves it when the kids come out to play.

We sometimes go out on a walk,
You'd swear my dog could even talk.
She loves to run and jump about,
I don't often have to scream and shout.

I love my dog more than I can say,
She shows me each and every day.
Don't be scared when she's around
She'll lie down for a tickle and not make a sound.

Chloe Sproston (7)
Kingsley St John's CE Primary School, Kingsley

Hunger

Blue is the colour of a deep, dark, empty ocean
with green, greasy seaweed.
It sounds like wavy blue waves
floating to the shore.
It smells like lovely smoky bacon
with saucy sauce on the tasty top.
It feels wetter than a waterfall splashing on the stones.
It makes me feel like I am in the middle of nowhere.

Marcus Alexander Lythgoe (8)
Kingsley St John's CE Primary School, Kingsley

Laughter

Blue is the colour of laughter like a burst water pipe
                                        that has fired up in the air
And someone is floating on.
It sounds like a river with rapids that stretch for miles.
It tastes like a funny, bitter taste.
It smells like pepper that makes you sneeze.
It reminds me of water falling from a cloud.
It makes me feel funny.

Tom Waring (8)
Kingsley St John's CE Primary School, Kingsley

Darkness

Black is the colour of the night sky.
The sound is like someone screeching.
The taste is an evil taste that makes you want to faint.
The smell is like an explosion of darkness
And it reminds me of being in bed with darkness creeping around
And I don't like it because it is scary.

Alex Daugan (9)
Kingsley St John's CE Primary School, Kingsley

Darkness

Red is like the colour of blood.
Black is like the colour of dark cellars.
It sounds like a lion's roar.
It tastes like cold pancakes that I hate.
It smells like a torture house.
It feels like a dark, sticky liquid.
It reminds me of someone that's mean to me.
I don't like it, it makes me feel creepy.

Alexander Palfreyman (8)
Kingsley St John's CE Primary School, Kingsley

Fear

Red like the colour of lava
It sounds like an earthquake
The smell is like a hot pepper
It tastes like a burnt chicken
It looks like a dragon coming to life
I feel I am going to burst into flames.

Daniel Steen (8)
Kingsley St John's CE Primary School, Kingsley

Fear

Fear is red like the colour of dark blood,
It sounds like a plane screeching across the sky,
The smell is angry and it makes me feel sick,
It tastes like very hot curry that burns your mouth,
It feels very tough and rough like grain,
It reminds me of a roller coaster,
I do not like it because it screams and hurts your ears.

Matthew Thomas Lythgoe (8)
Kingsley St John's CE Primary School, Kingsley

Anger

It is like a lion touching me and biting me all of the time.
It reminds me of my sister slamming doors and stamping around.
It makes me feel like I am in World War II.
Red is the colour of anger like fire from a dragon.
It sounds like twenty rhinos charging down a fence.
A weird taste that makes me want to spit out.
A nasty smell that I would run away from.

Oliver Cartwright (7)
Kingsley St John's CE Primary School, Kingsley

Anger

Red is the colour of *anger* like an erupting volcano spitting out lava.
Anger sounds like a bomb crashing into a house.
The taste is like a fire in my stomach that can't be put out.
The smell is like the burning of leaves.
It feels like a very hot burning rock.
It reminds me of my deadly sister.
I don't like it, it makes me feel like I am hurt inside.

Nina Atkinson (9)
Kingsley St John's CE Primary School, Kingsley

Happiness

Sky-blue is the colour of *happiness* like a sunny sky.
It sounds like laughter.
It tastes like a scrumptious taste that makes you want more.
The smell is like pancakes cooking in the pan.
The touch feels like fluffy clouds high in the sky.
It reminds me of my birthday.

Rachael Faint (8)
Kingsley St John's CE Primary School, Kingsley

Anger

Red is the colour of the roaring fire raging out of control.
It sounds like drums banging loudly at a busy rock concert.
It tastes like hot spicy curry that burns your mouth.
The smell is of burnt pizza that makes you hold your nose.
It feels like a thorn bush with rough spikes that prick you.

Elliot Rowe (8)
Kingsley St John's CE Primary School, Kingsley

Hate

Red is the colour of blood,
It sounds like someone wailing,
It tastes cold, it would freeze my mouth,
It smells like a great big ball of flesh
And when you touch it, you can feel brains,
It reminds me of when I broke my nose.

Robbie Conduit (8)
Kingsley St John's CE Primary School, Kingsley

What Is . . . The Ice?

The ice is a frosty car
sliding across the motorway

The ice is more slippery than sliding
down a fireman's pole

The ice is a clear glass window
under my feet

The ice is a sandy coloured lion
roaring in the sky.

Curtis Lowe (10)
Monton Green Primary School, Eccles

What Is . . . The Rain?

The rain is a teardrop
that shall never stop.

The rain is glitter
which is shiny but not bitter.

The rain is a whale
jumping with a whale
to catch a fish to eat.

The rain is huge rings
that are from the kings.

The rain is a mean queen
that makes it rain
she's just a pain.

The rain is crystals falling down
and when the crystals come there'll be no more frowns.

Mia Grundy (10)
Monton Green Primary School, Eccles

What Is . . . The Snow?

The snow is a melted slush of ice,
under my feet on the cold floor.

The snow is ice cream,
very cold when it goes in my mouth.

The snow is a string of wool
falling from the sky.

The snow is vanilla
melting as you lick it with your tongue.

The snow is a hailstone
falling down to the ground.

The snow is a white feather
falling down on my hand.

Reema Kadir (10)
Monton Green Primary School, Eccles

What Is . . . The Snow?

Snow falls from the high winter sky,
the people say oh my, oh my.

Snow is cold,
but it never gets old.

Snow will freeze,
when Santa comes on Christmas Eve.

Snow will be found,
next to a shiny golden pound.

Snow is really mucky,
compared to a Slush Puppie.

Snow is ice cream,
it might just make you want to scream!

Snow falls on trees,
it might just make you want to bow on your knees.

Billy Swindells (9)
Monton Green Primary School, Eccles

What Is . . . The Rain?

The rain is like
falling teardrops
dripping down
the cloud's face.

The rain is like lava
drifting down
the volcanoes.

The rain is like
falling rocks
splashing in the sea
like hailstones.

The rain is like a dolphin
jumping in the sea
to catch Nemo.

Danielle Hudson (10)
Monton Green Primary School, Eccles

Nature!

The fox in the water, not a sound not a stir,
as quiet as a cat sleeping while he purrs.

The fish in the water, the fish in the sea,
beautiful and colourful just like you and me.

Butterflies fly as I go by,
beautiful colours to my eye.

It's winter now, the snow is falling,
Jack Frost will soon be calling.

Children are making snowballs in the park,
making snowmen as it gets dark.

There's no leaves on the trees
there's icicles instead, but not to worry
the tree is not dead.

Ice is silvery and white,
but sometimes you can get frostbite.

Polar bears are white as a cloud,
but sometimes are a little loud.

Amy Foy (10)
Monton Green Primary School, Eccles

Loudly!

Loudly the planes roar across the land,
Loudly the children play on the sand.
Loudly the lion roars about,
Loudly the baby screams and shouts.
Loudly the bullets come out of a gun,
Loudly the elephants stampede and run!
Loudly the giant stamps like mad,
Loudly the child cries, he's sad.
Loudly the adults slam the door,
Loudly the children stamp on the floor.

Georgia Fisher (10)
Monton Green Primary School, Eccles

What Is . . . The Snow?

The snow is a white fluffy cloud,
That falls to the ground.

The snow is very small
And sticks to the wall.

The snow can change shape,
Even into a cape.

The snow is freezing,
But it will never start sneezing.

The snow is in the North Pole,
It will always be in your soul.

The snow will start freezing,
On Christmas evening.

The snow can change into a big snowman,
Build one if you can.

It turns into a stormy blizzard,
You never know it might be a lizard.

Nathan Noble (9)
Monton Green Primary School, Eccles

What Is . . . A Snow Blizzard?

A snow blizzard is
a man swiftly sprinting to the shops.

A snow blizzard is
a cloud of hail that never stops.

A snow blizzard is
like a box of popcorn that randomly pops.

A snow blizzard is
a map moving from side to side.

Joshua Gary Allan Brooks (9)
Monton Green Primary School, Eccles

What Is . . . The Snow?

The snow is an ice cream
white and cold.

> The snow is drops of sugar
> falling from the sky.

The snow is tissue ripped
up into pieces.

> The snow is a towel
> rolled up into a ball.

Jack Oliver Stott (9)
Monton Green Primary School, Eccles

What Is . . . The Snow?

The snow is a white fluffy cloud.
The snow falls like a roller coaster speeding down.

The snow falls from the sky that is very high.
When the snow falls you should play in the snow.

The snow is an ice cream cone.
The snow is a polar bear in the cold.

Jordan Hamilton (9)
Monton Green Primary School, Eccles

Ice

Ice is like a piece of chocolate melting in your mouth
Softly and smoothly.
Ice is frozen snowballs falling and sinking under the sea.
Ice is see-through and shatters when it breaks.
Ice is socks falling from the sky.
Ice is a window of glass falling.
Ice is a big huge sheet covering a seat.

Olivia Garey (10)
Monton Green Primary School, Eccles

The Snow

The snow is a polar bear
That swipes at doors
And rattles the trees
Breaking laws

He rushes around
Hidden in the night
Making sure
There is no light

When he hits
The icy floor
He will shout
Roar, roar, roar

People were walking
Home from school
As they noticed
There an icy pool

As he settles
Lying down
He is as still as
The Queen's crown

When he goes to sleep
He's still like a polar bear
Circling you with an icy stare.

Julian Millidge (10)
Monton Green Primary School, Eccles

What Is . . . The Snow?

The snow was coming down as hard as basketballs
The snow looks like Santa's beard
The snow is cold like a freezer
The people were shivering when the snow hit them.

Declan Tasker
Monton Green Primary School, Eccles

The Tiger Breaks Free

Behind the dreaded silver bars,
The car park is full of cars.
The tiger has been there for years and years
Its smooth soft fur covering its ears is going rough
The tiger has had enough!

At the break of day
The tiger rises
He is going to leave some big surprises.

The zookeeper wakes to feed the tiger
As well as the zoo's liger.
But when he gets there the tiger's gone,
In that place the sun once shone.
It shone like millions of tiny lights
Next the zookeeper got some frights.
All the animals had left their cage,
How would the zookeeper pay his wage?

Meanwhile, the animals were in the town,
A monkey had stolen a shiny crown.
The penguin was wearing a bra,
The elephant was driving a car.
The giraffe's head was stuck in a window,
Just from trying to do the limbo.
The zebra was looking at all the sights,
A crocodile was staring at the traffic lights.

'Will it ever end?' cried the zookeeper
'No,' laughed the zoo's orange and stripy creature.

Abbie Dickens (11)
Monton Green Primary School, Eccles

What Is . . . The Snow?

The snow is a slushy melted piece of ice.
The snow is a mushy scoop of rice pudding.
The snow is a cold rug on the concrete.
The snow is cold milk smudged across the floor.

Jodie Macauley (9)
Monton Green Primary School, Eccles

What Is . . . The Snow?

The snow is a soft and fluffy slush.
The snow is smashed up ice.

The snow is cold and mushy rice pudding in a very cold bowl.
The snow is mushed up ice cream.

The snow is crushed up pasta that is very cold.
The snow is a mushy yoghurt.

It is a ball of crushed up ice.
The snow is a soft white blanket.

Abbie Lauren Staunton
Monton Green Primary School, Eccles

What Is . . . The Ice?

Ice is a glass sheet over a car.
If ice falls off it will shatter.

Ice is as cold as snow.
Ice is as cold as a fridge.

Ice is as see-through as glass.
Ice is as see-through as a window.

Ryan Boothman
Monton Green Primary School, Eccles

The Snow!

The snow is a bunch of gold-white blankets
just being on the floor bright and light

Snow is a cloud rushing from the sky

Snow is a biscuit crunching under your feet

Snow is a silver penny lying on the floor.

Dean Hadcock (10)
Monton Green Primary School, Eccles

What Is . . . The Snow?

The snow is a soft white polar bear
in the Arctic.

The snow is a fluffy white cloud
in the sky.

The snow is a giant rug
covering the North Pole.

The snow is a cuddly Arctic fox
settling in for a snooze.

The snow is a soft white cat
jumping off a wall.

The snow is a snowman
melting into white chocolate.

Jade Leah Brandreth (9)
Monton Green Primary School, Eccles

The Snow

The snow is a bear
He roars in rage
He smashes the bars
And rattles the cage.

He runs through trees
And swipes and screeches
Tall as a house
Fast as a cheetah
He circles the town
He scampers around
He lurches through wind
And falls to the ground.

He settles down calmly
He lies on house tops
Covering the world
He flops, he flops.

Josh Williamson (11)
Monton Green Primary School, Eccles

The Snow

The snow is a polar bear
That knocks at doors
And rocks windows
With its paws.

Hidden in the night
He rushes around
Looking for the houses
Making angry sounds.

Tired the next morning
Dawdling around
Scratching himself
He sits down on the ground.

He quietly walks away
You hardly notice him go
Trampling on cars
To find another place to blow.

Jessica Lawson (11)
Monton Green Primary School, Eccles

The Snow

The snow is a knight
That charges down doors
And smashes windows
With his sword.

Hidden in the night
He loiters around
Waiting for prey
To bring to the ground.

With his sword
He knocks down cattle
He settles and saves
His power at the breach of battle.

Connor Brownbill (10)
Monton Green Primary School, Eccles

The Countryside

The countryside is peaceful, as quiet as a mouse,
You can see the farmer amble from house to house.
The wheat sways as though it is a vast crowd
Listening to a slow song at Live 8,
The cows' refreshing milk is delivered in a nice blue milk crate.

The small, thatched cottages are packed together like peas in a pod,
The extensive sunflowers are like an extreme fishing rod.
Cows and sheep dotted around the field,
Working horses as strong as a Roman shield.

The big brown fence as long as a railway track,
The small storage barns are back to back.
Countryside streams, narrow, shallow and long,
With sweet birds above singing a serene song.

The countryside is a fantastic place to live,
With everyone there willing to give.
So come and enjoy a fantastic life,
With peaceful things in the countryside.

Jonathon Smith (11)
Monton Green Primary School, Eccles

Thunder

The thunder is a gorilla
That punches doors
And smashes windows
With his big fists.

Hidden in the trees
He stomps around
The protected house
Making ferocious roars.

He swings from vines onto the roof
He lashes out his roar
And people get horrified
To the pit of their stomach.

Jake Rogers (10)
Monton Green Primary School, Eccles

Animals

Animals come in all shapes and sizes;
some of them bear precious prizes.
Snakes and vipers are green,
lions are terribly mean.
Leopards are as lean and sleek as a log,
rabbits hop like a frog.
Elephants are big and grey;
wolves have nothing but *aawhoo* to say.
The cheetah was running so fast,
you'd think his spots would come off at last.
Poachers shoot animals even though it's illegal,
they mostly shoot rhino and sometimes eagle.
There's only one type of animal that thinks cheese is nice
and of course it could only be mice!

Matthew Anns (10)
Monton Green Primary School, Eccles

Dogs

Dogs can be as big as a mountain or as small as a mouse,
Dogs live in the wild or in somebody's house,
Dogs pull and pull with all their might until you fall,
Dogs love to play with a ball.

Dogs are all different colours, red, yellow and blue,
Whatever colour they are, they will always love you!

Some dogs are strong, some dogs are weak,
Some dogs' fur is rough and some are sleek,
Some dogs are tall and some are short,
Some dogs are quiet, some dogs are loud and some even snort!
Some people like them that much they have three, four or five!

Dogs, dogs, dogs, the greatest creatures alive!

Ryan Maybury (10)
Monton Green Primary School, Eccles

Dancing

The dancing shoes are as sparkly as a glass slipper.
The skirts are as long as a diver's flipper.

The outfits are as clingy as a chimpanzee on its mother's back.
If you do well you will win a plaque.

The music is as graceful as a swan on a lake.
You've got to be careful not to flake.

The salsa is as spicy as a tub of salsa dip.
You'd better not make a blip.

The tango has a lot of attitude.
Pretend to be in an angry mood.

Stamp your feet like you just don't care.
Never mind what you want to wear.

One day you will be out of breath.
Be careful you don't dance to death!

Samantha Wright (11)
Monton Green Primary School, Eccles

The Sea

The sea sparkles like a sapphire in bright daylight,
the sun lights up the top of the sea as if it's swimming,
the waves surge and lunge forward like a burning inferno.

Shark skin is sleek and smooth,
coral is rough and tough,
dolphins can jump colossally high,
whales are fat, full of blubber,
their skin feels like a tyre of rubber.

Jack Haslam (10)
Monton Green Primary School, Eccles

Art

Art is where you let your imagination flow,
when you have an idea let your pen go.
Modelling with clay and drawing with paint,
tip over water and it becomes faint.

Art is a skill you will never forget,
it is also a skill you will never regret.
When it rains like a giant's crying
and you have nothing to do,
get some paint and a piece of paper or two
and draw, draw, draw!

It does not matter how you draw,
even if you think it's poor.
You have developed your special style,
as special as the River Nile.

The more you practise with paint and clay,
The bigger chance you will become an artist someday!

Lucy Wharton (10)
Monton Green Primary School, Eccles

Pandas

Two pandas lived in China,
for them there was no place finer.
Plodding along like it was all they could do,
but it wasn't, they could do a few.
Sleeping at night,
playing during the day.
Climbing colossal trees,
now they're free they do as they please.
As the day dawns,
the sun soars.
As they watch, it warms their hearts,
red, orange and yellow, so lovely but just the start!

Alexandra Clifford (10)
Monton Green Primary School, Eccles

Animals!

The dog sleeps as silent as a star in the night
rolling around in his warm place,
as the day breaks out he's ready to fight
slowly and calmly he keeps his pace.

The birds fly as gracefully as the swan on the lake
swooping through bushes and trees,
as the shy red breast sings and hops on the rake
but the birds stay clear of the buzzing bees.

Giraffes have tall, smooth necks, long, thin and spotty
with hair all short and stubbly,
baby giraffes are small, cute and bubbly
cute enough to drive you dotty!

A horse's skin is as soft as a sheep
soft, furry and gentle,
horses also gallop, trot and leap
but if there's a loud noise the horse goes mental!

Natasha Naylor (10)
Monton Green Primary School, Eccles

Australia

When you walk down the road, you could burn your feet,
Quivering, trembling in the tremendous heat.
Australia is the place to be,
White sandy beaches and sapphire-blue sea.

You can choose to visit the Sydney Opera House,
Or the breathtaking Ayres Rock, as quiet as a mouse.
Ride around Melbourne city on the infamous tram,
Stop off at the deli, for a delicious salad sandwich with ham.

The Great Barrier Reef is waiting for you,
So hop on a plane and I'll see you soon!

Eliza Crosara (10)
Monton Green Primary School, Eccles

The Referee's Whistle!

I have to blow my whistle many times,
So I will describe those situations to you in this rhyme.
When I blow my whistle loud,
The players scream just like the crowd.
When a player places the ball down,
Nobody makes a sound.
The loudest team I've ever seen,
Are the Pompey boys; barmy and lean.

I enjoy penalty shootouts you see;
Great drama and no pressure on me.
I've now got to referee a game,
To stop me from going insane.

Jonathan Barrett (9)
Monton Green Primary School, Eccles

Animals

I walk my dog in the dark,
when he sees others of his kind he lets out a very big bark.

The cheetah runs like there is no tomorrow,
if you get in his way you are sure of sorrow.

The giraffe walks tall above all,
he eats the leaves on the very tall trees.

The monkey swings low, the monkey swings high
they are so fast they might just nick your tie.

When an elephant walks around,
it feels like the world is turning upside down.

A snake is as skinny as a stick,
but when you get near it don't try a trick.

Joseph Morrissy (9)
Monton Green Primary School, Eccles

Night Creature

Its tail is like a witch's broom,
It comes out when it sees the moon.
It creeps in the wood to catch its prey,
It hides again at the break of day.

Now the sun is in the air,
It's hidden away with its reddish hair.
It waits expectantly for creatures to appear,
It sniffs and smells, something is near!

And there lays a little hen,
So it comes out once again.
It looks and stares with its meanish face,
As it chases with so much pace.

Because the creature lost the hen,
It solemnly returned to its den.
The hen got away and hid near a box,
So the creature must have been a very sly fox!

Daniella Johnston (11)
Monton Green Primary School, Eccles

Rapidly

Rapidly the cobra spits its venom,
Rapidly the juice squirts from a lemon.

Rapidly the bullet shoots from a gun,
Rapidly the athlete goes for a run.

Rapidly the lightning strikes from the sky,
Rapidly the spider catches a fly.

Rapidly the race car leaves the pit stop,
Rapidly the new CDs are bought from the shop.

Rapid is a cheetah, but most rapid by far
Are the spinning wheels on a Porsche sports car.

James Woodward (11)
Monton Green Primary School, Eccles

Danny!

D is for *dreamy*
A is for *amazing*
N is for *never lets his fans down*
N is for *never gives up*
Y is for *young and famous*

You play gigs all year through,
People pay to come and watch you,
They dance and sing
They scream and shout
They can't stop moving their bodies about!

Georgia Page (10)
Monton Green Primary School, Eccles

My Magical Dream

In my dream I could see . . .
A man made of milk chocolate.
I was going to eat him
But he was nice to me
And he was kind.

I could hear . . .
The frozen apple juice birds
Floating above me,
Flapping their beautiful wings
As I lay sleeping in the garden.

In my dreams I could imagine . . .
The world was edible,
I wish I could eat
The sweet sparkly leaves
Off the bushes and trees.
I wish it would come true.

Ja-Leigh Astles (8)
Murdishaw West Community Primary School, Murdishaw

The Magical Dream

In my dream I could see . . .
My palace waiting for me.
A throne for my seat.
A seat at the top of the table just for me.

I could hear . . .
My delicious dinner cooking.
My servant bringing me a morning drink.
My children running and shouting to me.
My mother calling me.

I could imagine . . .
Me growing old,
Just my family and me.

I wish it could come true.

Kenniann Grainger (8)
Murdishaw West Community Primary School, Murdishaw

Beautiful Dreams

In my dream I could see . . .
Fairies dancing and sparkling as they moved,
They were softly talking.

In my dream I could hear . . .
The children laughing and singing,
As they walked home
They seemed so happy.

In my dream I could feel . . .
The soft breeze in my hair as I walked.
It was very beautiful.
What a dream.

Georgia Mawdsley (9)
Murdishaw West Community Primary School, Murdishaw

The Impossible Dream

In my dream I could hear . . .
My pet dog talking to me,
Faintly saying, 'I am hungry.'

I could hear . . .
Birds singing with astonishing words.

In my dream I could see . . .
Unicorns flying around
With angels on their backs.

In my dream I could imagine . . .
Me, the princess of this crazy land
And every ogre of greed praising me
With dancing flowers.

Is this crazy land real
Or is this just a dream?

Jessica Smith (8)
Murdishaw West Community Primary School, Murdishaw

The Dragon Parade

I see the lucky envelopes hanging
and the dragon pinching them from window to window.
I hear the roaring of the dragon
as he dances through the parade.
I feel the excitement as the dragon roars with anger.
I smell the burning of the crackers
as they shoot and light the night sky with wonder.
I taste the lovely Chinese food
as the dragon dances around.
I am the Chinese dragon.

Anna Johnson (8)
Murdishaw West Community Primary School, Murdishaw

My Poet's Dream

In my dream I could see . . .
Someone walking in the park,
The leaves were rustling in the wind
And it was very cold.

In my dream I could hear . . .
A man shouting at someone
And he or she was shouting back.

In my dream I could imagine . . .
That there was a girl
And I was standing there,
Just staring, then she ran away,
From somebody that I didn't know.

Rebekkah Fearns-Pugh (8)
Murdishaw West Community Primary School, Murdishaw

My Amazing Dream

In my dream I could see . . .
A huge cheetah stomping through my school,
Running, charging, chasing us.

In my dream I could hear . . .
The roaring, screeching of the cheetah,
The screaming, shouting of everyone else.

In my dream I could feel . . .
My heart pounding
Because I was scared,
The floor was shaking,
My feet were quaking.

Abigail Prescott (9)
Murdishaw West Community Primary School, Murdishaw

The Impossible Dream

In my dream I could hear . . .
The roaring of Simba the lion
And the calling of the lion's mate Nala.

In my dream I could see . . .
The speed of the tiger running
And the trembling of the cheetah,
They are having a race.

In my dream I could hear . . .
The trembling of a leaf
As it shakes on a branch in the wind.

Marc Stoddart (8)
Murdishaw West Community Primary School, Murdishaw

Fairy-Tale Dream

In my dream I could hear . . .
The pixies chatting
And singing a lively tune.

In my dream I could see . . .
The giant getting fatter
From all those chickens he's eaten.

In my dream I could almost feel . . .
The fairy's wings
Beating against my excited face.

I wish this could come true.

Demi-Lee Hatfield (9)
Murdishaw West Community Primary School, Murdishaw

The Chinese New Year

I can see Lord Buddha walking down the road.
I hear the happiness of children laughing.
I feel my heart banging in time with the drums.
I smell the people burning the firecrackers.
I taste the food I have bought in the street.
I am the Chinese dragon on the long road to China.

Matthew Holmes (9)
Murdishaw West Community Primary School, Murdishaw

Chinese Dragon

I see the shiny cymbals crashing in the sunlight.
I hear the stamping of the dragon's feet.
I feel scared and excited when the dragon comes near.
I smell delicious Chinese food.
I taste noodles in a tangy sauce.
I am the Chinese dragon.

Lewis Jackson (9)
Murdishaw West Community Primary School, Murdishaw

Chinese Code

I see the Chinese dragon dancing.
I smell the firecracker's smoke.
I hear the stamping of the dragon's claws.
I feel excited before I climb into the dragon's costume, I am the head.
I taste lucky fortune cookies.
I am the Chinese dragon.

Oliver Preece (8)
Murdishaw West Community Primary School, Murdishaw

The Kitten

Playing non-stop,
The kitten is always awake.
Jumping wildly,
Up and down the creaking stairs.

Running endlessly,
Round the frost-covered garden.
Leaping, catching,
Digging in the flowerbeds.

Yawning sleepily,
The kitten finds her bed.
Cosy, warm,
The kitten is fast asleep.

Josie McLaughlin (10)
Nevill Road Junior School, Bramhall

What Is Red?

What is red? A rose is red,
As it grows in the summer bed.

What is red? Blood is red,
From the body of someone dead.

What is red? A sunset is red,
As you look at it from your bed.

What is red? An angry face is red,
Just like when all the blood rushes to your head.

What is red? Jam is red,
To spread on your buttered bread.

What is red? Sunburn is red,
Let's stay covered up instead.

Christopher Gration (10)
Nevill Road Junior School, Bramhall

This Is The Night When Witches Fly

Tonight is the night when witches fly.
On their whizzing broomstick
Through the dark and misty sky.
Racing up the pathway where the stars are strewn.
They stretch their bony fingers up to the dazzling moon.
This is the night when they say, 'Trick or treat?'
You'll get scared stiff from your head to your feet.
'Oh no!' you cry,
For you have seen the true meaning of Hallowe'en.

Katie Jeffers (8)
Nevill Road Junior School, Bramhall

Tropical Poem

I can see snakes swirling around me.
I can see seagulls swooping in the air.
I can feel seaweed tangled up around my feet
And sand in my toes.
I can hear waves going up and down.
I can hear people screaming so loud
And I can smell fish in the sea.

Tom Belsham (7)
Nevill Road Junior School, Bramhall

A Beautiful Dolphin

Dolphins swimming in the day,
Playing in the water with their friends.
They say and say, 'Let's play!'
When they jump they shine.
Dolphins chasing, three in a row,
Swirling, diving like part of a show.
Sparkly eyes and a big, friendly grin.
A beautiful animal, a lovely dolphin.

Terri Lau (8)
Nevill Road Junior School, Bramhall

Sunflowers

Sunflowers, sunflowers rising from the ground
Sunflowers, sunflowers they are all around
With fluffy bees and singing birds
Just love to play with what they have found.

Sunflowers, sunflowers with bright yellow petals
Gleaming through the long wide fields
With flowers and seeds scattered about
Are all planted here for the birds to feed.

The sun is warm, the breeze is fresh
People playing until dawn
All day long we run and jump
Finding ways to enjoy the day.

As the day ends
The sun fades away
Out pops the dark night and cold breeze
And settles for another day.

Gabriella Benincasa (8)
Nevill Road Junior School, Bramhall

What Is Red?

What is red? Blood is red,
Pumping round inside your head.

What is red? Raw steak is red,
The food on which lions are fed.

What is red? Sundown is red,
Keeping us warm before we go to bed.

What is red? Traffic lights are red,
The car stopped because the traffic light said.

What is red? Mars is red,
Nothing lives there because the planet is dead.

Jack Rushton (10)
Nevill Road Junior School, Bramhall

Believe

I had no friends and my mind was bleak
I was looking into the sea when I heard a squeak
It was a dolphin, it was so pretty
I was stroking a kitty
I asked it its name.
'Magic,' it said.
I left Magic and went to bed.
In the morning I went to see
If Magic was waiting for me
I played with him in the sea
I fed him a pea
I showed him to my sister
All she was interested in was her giant blister
So from that day I knew I had to believe
In magic to see him.
So you have to believe in magic to see things others can't.

Sophie Harrison (10)
Nevill Road Junior School, Bramhall

What Is Red?

What is red? Spots are red,
Dotting around all over my head.

What is red? Roses are red,
Sleeping by the garden bed.

What is red? Evil eyes are red,
Popping out of my teacher's head.

What is red? Jam is red,
To spread on toast and eat in bed.

What is red? Apples are red,
'They're good for you,' my mum said.

Molly Bridge (10)
Nevill Road Junior School, Bramhall

What Is Green?

What is green? Leaves are green,
On a tree that can be seen.

What is green? Traffic lights are green,
All together in a team.

What is green? Apples are green,
With little pips in-between.

What is green? Grass is green,
Grass is where I grow my beans.

What is green? The classroom carpet is green,
Smells all musty and unclean.

Ben Blackburn (9)
Nevill Road Junior School, Bramhall

Friendship Simile Poem

A good friend is as truthful as God.
My friend is precious like a ruby.
Friends are as caring as a dove.
A good friend is as helpful as a light.
My friend is as wise as an owl.
Friends are as sweet as sugar.

Harriet Lomax (9)
Nevill Road Junior School, Bramhall

My Friend

My friend is as wise as the three kings.
My friend is as nice as chocolate.
My friend is as friendly as my dad.
My friend is as helpful as my mum.
My friend sings like a bird.
My friend howls like a wolf.

Alexander Jenkinson (8)
Nevill Road Junior School, Bramhall

What Is Blue?

What is blue? A shoe is blue
Worn by who?

What is blue? The sea is blue
That welcomes you.

What is blue? The sky is blue
And birds fly in the white clouds too.

What is blue? Eeyore is blue
And friends with Winnie the Pooh.

What is blue? Eyes are blue
That stare at you.

Fayth McCormick (10)
Nevill Road Junior School, Bramhall

Playful Dolphins

Playful dolphins swimming in the waves
Playful dolphins are so brave
Playful dolphins in the ocean
Playful dolphins dancing in motion.

Playful dolphins, can they see me?
Playful dolphins, can it be?
Playful dolphins have a good fin
Playful dolphins have a brilliant win.

Joshua Walsh (9)
Nevill Road Junior School, Bramhall

Under The Sea

Plunging straight down under the sea.
Falling down into an octopus' garden.
The octopus floats as light as a blanket.
Wandering around the seabed with their friends.

Dominic Gamble (9)
Nevill Road Junior School, Bramhall

Coral Reef

Under the water
Where no one has been
A lot of colourful treasures
Crimson-red, sapphire-blue
Racing-green, golden yellow
And chocolate-brown.

All of this glory
Is under the sea
Fish hide in them
Got to get away
Into the colour
No one can find you.

It looks like an underwater garden
Where if you step on it
You will go right through it
And have a nasty shock
You will have broken it.

Luke Thomas (9)
Nevill Road Junior School, Bramhall

Dancing Shoes

Twirling and swirling and spinning around
I'm flying so high, so far from the ground,
Dancing shoes on my feet
How I feel so alive, going so high into the blue sky,
Watching the birds as they fly gently by.
Then slowly and gently without a sound,
I float like a leaf softly back to the ground,
With not a care in the world I look to the ground
To find upon my feet my dream that I have found,
My dancing shoes that sparkle
Through the love that I have found.

Georgia Murray (8)
Nevill Road Junior School, Bramhall

The Shark

She swims around ferociously,
Searching for her next meal,
Her dark fins close around a seal,
The blood spurts out,
The flesh, fresh but soaked,
A dark red blanket.
The blue salty water scattered
With skin, bones and the dark smell of death.

Fish huddle together like a large orange ball,
Running down the path.
She swims around randomly
Resting on every rock.
The sea, a protection for every sea creature
As she swims around,
The queen of the sea,
Her jaws slice together like a knife.
She carries the smell of death.

Jessy Dixon (10)
Nevill Road Junior School, Bramhall

What Is Blue?

What is blue? A bluebell is blue,
Glistening in the morning dew.

What is blue? Ink is blue,
For writing a mystery clue.

What is blue? The sky is blue,
As bright as if brand new.

What is blue? The sea is blue,
Admired by a ship's crew.

What is blue? A blue jay is blue,
Calling down to you.

Tom Callan (10)
Nevill Road Junior School, Bramhall

Under The Sea

Deeper and deeper,
Down in the big blue,
To a wet world
And to see the things that fishes do,
An underwater garden,
Where the creatures float,
Flowing through the water,
Swishing past with their shiny coat,
Admiring their cosy seabed,
Silent like Heaven's peace,
Little fishes resting their heads,
Searching the sea,
By the coral,
All fishes in bed under the sea.

Jonathan Law (9)
Nevill Road Junior School, Bramhall

What Is Blue?

What is blue? The sky is blue
With a fluffy cloud or two.

What is blue? A car is blue
Travelling so fast it almost flew.

What is blue? The sea is blue
The tide came in and speedily grew.

What is blue? My duvet is blue
Warm and cosy to sleep like you.

What is blue? A blueberry is blue
Sweet and juicy, you start to chew.

Teigan Bancroft (9)
Nevill Road Junior School, Bramhall

The Hare And The Tortoise

There once was a really fast hare,
Who could beat anyone who dared,
To try and beat him in a race,
But he would always win
And boast in their face!
Then came a tortoise with a very good voice
Who challenged the hare to a long race.
'It's not possible for him to win,' said Monkey
Who in fact was very, very chunky.
As the race went ahead as planned,
Bang! went the starting gun.
The very long race started
And the hare dashed ahead as usual,
But the hare soon got tired
And decided very quickly
That he would have a quick nap
But knowing his luck he had overslept
And the tortoise crept over him quietly.
After a while the hare woke up
Looked at the time and had a shock
And his body shook like a trunk,
He dashed and he dived to the finishing line
But the tortoise was already there
And was sitting on the winner's chair.
Finally the hare was beaten
For it had also been found
That he had been cheating,
So the hare never boasted again!

Curtis Volp (9)
Nevill Road Junior School, Bramhall

What Is Pink?

What is pink? My room is pink
In my room I always think.

What is pink? My bed is pink
On my bed I spilt some ink.

What is pink? My bobble is pink
When I wear it, it makes the boys wink.

What is pink? My TV is pink
When I watch it, it makes me blink.

What is pink? My drink's pink
My favourite drink is from a sink.

Alice Burden (9)
Nevill Road Junior School, Bramhall

The Peter Pan Poem

There once was a girl called Wendy
Who wanted to go away.
Peter Pan came from high in the sky
And said, 'Come on girl, let's go away.'
So they went away to Neverland.
They went to see the boys
The funny little lot
And saw their best friend Captain Hook
And talked and talked
And had a good time.
They went back home
And partied all night with food and drink
Waiting for something good to begin.

Rosaria D'agostino (10)
Nevill Road Junior School, Bramhall

Under The Sea

Different blues for different seas
Waves crashing like white horses leaping
Deeper and deeper down we go
Treasures
Coral, as precious as a treasure chest
Colourful
Salty fingers stretching out
Seaweed in all shades of green
A sea horse as pretty as a mermaid
Mermaid maze
A lost forest
Rainbow-coloured fish
Skeleton trees.

Eilish Frost (9)
Nevill Road Junior School, Bramhall

What Is Red?

What is red? The heart of love
Is like a flying dove.

What is red? A strawberry
Eaten with cream with tea.

What is red? The sun as it sets
Like a man and woman who just met.

What is red? A ruby
That glitters and also boogies.

What is red? A heart
Pierced with Cupid's dart.

Anouska Webb (9)
Nevill Road Junior School, Bramhall

I'm A Gorilla

I'm a gorilla
I thump my chest
To let you know who's boss
Down in the jungle
They all keep clear
When they hear that I am cross

I'm a gorilla
I'm covered in fur
With silver down my back
I'm as big as a man
But as strong as ten
I'm the leader of the pack

I'm a gorilla
I eat my fruit
I also like a bug
I can pick up trees
And pick my own fleas

But I do love a great big hug!

Indy Taylor (7)
Nevill Road Junior School, Bramhall

Reindeer

I am a reindeer, big and tough,
I trot around in the tundra rough.
I eat grass, covered in crispy snow,
Which helps to make my antlers grow.

I drink from streams with bobbing ice,
In summer I eat buds that taste nice.
I am used to pulling around sleighs and gigs,
I am a reindeer tough and big.

Charlotte Hyde (7)
Nevill Road Junior School, Bramhall

Bramhall Hall

Bramhall Hall is beautiful
Rich in treasures.
Amazing things can happen,
Maids are working.
Home is different,
All things are old.
Lots of things to see, do and say,
Like it so much.
Bramhall Hall,
Bramhall Hall,
Bramhall Hall,
Hey, watch the stairs,
All about the olden days,
Lucky rich people.
Lovely things to see!

Kyanna Moran-Cox (7)
Nevill Road Junior School, Bramhall

Summer

I can smell a sweet red rose
I can taste the grass that's mowed
I can feel the warm breeze
I can hear the summer bees.

With colours so bright
Gives my eyes a fright.

Buttercups, daffodils,
Cornflowers blue,
Which bit of summer
Is talking to you?

Emilia Troup (8)
Nevill Road Junior School, Bramhall

Storm

Illuminated sky . . . then suddenly
Dark clouds covering
Every trace of light.

People running
Panicking
Trying to find shelter.

Flash! Bang!
Thunder and lightning
Natural fireworks lighting the sky.

Rain, ambushing
The Earth
But never winning.

Rain, immense shower
Crashing against the window
Making me feel warm and cosy.

Then suddenly . . . illuminated sky.

Keir Birchall (11)
Nevill Road Junior School, Bramhall

What Is Blue?

What is blue? A Brazilian agate stone is blue
It has different hues.

What is blue? The sky is blue
On a sunny day, beautiful for you.

What is blue? A flower is blue
Planted, tended and watered it grew.

What is blue? My bag is blue
Which inside I have glue.

What is blue? My mum's coat is blue
You can get it in lots of different colours too.

Oliver Quinn (9)
Nevill Road Junior School, Bramhall

In Your Dreams

The referee blows the whistle, the game has started,
The 75,000 fans that have come to Stamford Bridge
Are in for a dream of a game,
Crespo to Makelele,
Great tackle by Bentley,
Bentley to McKenzie,
McKenzie runs, shoots, great save Petr Cech,
Cech to Lampard,
Robben dances down the wing
But gets tackled by Huckerby,
Huckerby runs and runs,
He crosses to Earnshaw,
Earnshaw shoots and scores!
Norwich City have beaten Chelsea in extra time,
Norwich are the champions of Europe.
'Wake up, wake up, Dale wake up!'
'Don't take me away from my dream, *nooooo!'*

Dale Whetter (10)
Nevill Road Junior School, Bramhall

Tropical Poem

Waves clashing together.
I can see the sunset resting on the rocks.
The shimmering sun.
Sand brushing everywhere on the top.
I can smell the sea water
I can smell the sea water.
I can hear the coconuts
I can hear the coconuts
Dropping from the trees
Dropping from the trees.
Warm breeze, you can feel the sea
And sand brushing against your legs.

Tessa Bridge (8)
Nevill Road Junior School, Bramhall

Tropical Poem

Monkeys swinging from trees
The smell of spice tingles my nose
The sun burns my back
The smell of spice tingles my nose
The rain cools me down
The smell of spice tingles my nose
I taste the dryness of the sun
The smell of spice tingles my nose
The dusty sand tickles my feet.

Harry Green (8)
Nevill Road Junior School, Bramhall

I Am The Sea

I am the sea, sometimes rough, sometimes calm.
I am the sea, people swim in me.
I am the sea, I crash against the wall.
I am the sea, I shiver and sparkle in the night.
I am the shivering sea.
I bubble in the night, sometimes in the day.
I am the sea, I am deep and sleek.
I am the sea, people get up bright and early
To come and swim in me.

Lauren Corbett (8)
Nevill Road Junior School, Bramhall

Dolphin Couplet Poem

Dolphin dancing in the blue sea
Twirling and twisting, looking at me
Beautiful skin shines in the sun
Gleaming and shines, having fun
Leaping over the ocean waves
Never scared, always brave.

Jasmine Barrett (9)
Nevill Road Junior School, Bramhall

The Beaches

You need the right clothes, head to toes
And suncream on your nose.
Seagulls are swooping down for fish,
Calm seas, lovely to swim in
And great views up high.
Thousands of people come every year.
Friendly people let you in
And fishes have a fin.
Rainy season can have bad hurricanes.

Bill Cann (8)
Nevill Road Junior School, Bramhall

Sea

Under the sea
As bright as can be
Fish swimming and dashing.
Under the sea
It's the best place you can be
Diving deeper and deeper.
Under the sea
It's as colourful as a gem
With sounds of bubbles popping
As a group of fish swim by.

Megan Crew-Meaney (8)
Nevill Road Junior School, Bramhall

Firework Descriptions

The bonfire is burning fast.
The flames are crackling.
The fire is roaring loudly.
The rocket goes *bang!* in the sky.
The Catherine wheels whizz around.

Sam Downs (9)
Nevill Road Junior School, Bramhall

Ring, Ring

Big and small
A telephone call
Much to say
Not much to pay
Girls and boys will
Laugh and say,
'Please, please
Will you come
Round to play?'

Amy Dutton (7)
Nevill Road Junior School, Bramhall

Dolphins Couplet Poem

Dolphins in the deep sea.
Wonderful sight to see.

Dolphins in the ocean
That go in slow motion.

Dolphins flick their tail
As they see a whale.

Dolphins leap out of the sea
As they want to be free.

Aimée Maynard-Smith (8)
Nevill Road Junior School, Bramhall

A Good Friend Is . . .

As gentle as the flapping of a butterfly's wings.
As special as the morning dew.
Like a new life.
Like a light in the shadows of evil.
As helpful as a lantern in the darkest graveyard.
As great as the Lord.

Toby White (9)
Nevill Road Junior School, Bramhall

Baby Animals

Kittens playing happily in the sunshine,
In the garden miaowing and whining.
Puppies fetching the ball back and forth,
Not knowing whether it's south or north.
Little bunnies, chubby and fat,
Afraid of animals like dogs or cats.
Scuttling hamsters, sweet and small,
Squeaking out that little tiny call.
A mini mouse, white with a long tail,
Tiny and small and very frail.
Terrapins, tiny with patterned shells,
All lined up in the shop ready to sell.
Monkeys swinging from tree to tree,
Swinging on so many trees, 1, 2, 3.
Patterned birds flying high in the air,
Flapping their wings without a care.
Big and hairy, a tiger cub,
The mum tiger rubs and scrubs.
Gold and shiny little fish,
Swimming round in a little goldfish dish.

Emily Connors (11)
Nevill Road Junior School, Bramhall

Whale Couplet Poem

I saw a whale under the sea,
Hunting for something for its tea.

I saw a whale under the sea,
I wanted to take it home with me.

I saw a whale under the sea,
Eating an octopus for its tea.

I saw a whale under the sea,
The biggest mammal in history.

Dominic Ciolfi (9)
Nevill Road Junior School, Bramhall

Under The Sea

Down we go under the sea,
Look over there, an underwater tree,
Look at the starfish lying on the floor,
Wait one second, here come more!
There are the crabs having a fight,
There's an angelfish, it gives off some light!
Wow, look at that, skull and bones,
Look at the flowers in all different zones.
Look at the flatfish swimming like that,
Look at the pufferfish, it's looking rather fat!
All these creatures, sea otters and all,
If you want more info just give me a call.

Jakob Williams (9)
Nevill Road Junior School, Bramhall

Dolphins Couplet Poem

What a beautiful sight
Still playing in the night.

Dolphins jump with a great big smile
You can hear them sing from a mile.

Making a wish
Chasing a fish.

Jumping in slow motion
Swimming under the ocean.

The dolphins have sharp minds
And they are very kind.

Silky smooth-looking skin
With a dorsal fin.

Sarah Green (9)
Nevill Road Junior School, Bramhall

The Monster

Not all monsters are cruel and spiteful,
Some are kind and quite delightful,
There is one monster in an ancient cave,
Who isn't evil and doesn't crave,
For flesh and bones and human blood,
This monster is extremely good,
He is crimson-red with purple spots
And loves all nature lots and lots.

Despite his huge and gleaming teeth,
He doesn't spend his time beneath
A bed; he would rather go swimming or be
Watching 'The Simpsons' on TV,
Whilst eating some soup and some veg,
Then going outside and cutting the hedge,
Not all monsters are cruel and spiteful,
Some are kind and quite delightful.

Lewis Ball (11)
Nevill Road Junior School, Bramhall

Dolphin Couplet Poem

What a wonderful thing to see
A dolphin swimming in the sea.

An amazing dolphin playing
While the waves are swaying.

Smiles with a cheeky grin
Proudly showing its fin.

What a playful creature
Acrobatics feature.

Swimming oh so very fast
Across oceans ships are passed.

Kieren Thompson (9) & Levi Roberts (8)
Nevill Road Junior School, Bramhall

These I Have Loved . . .

These I have loved . . .

Fire, amazingly flickering and dancing
With an intricate pattern to it,
Like a twirling bird of red, orange and yellow.
The sight of a beautiful sunset
Sinking through the darkening skies,
Like a golden ball falling back to Earth.
The lazy scent of lavender hushing me to sleep.
Wind; coldly brushing past me.
Exotic fruits - as many flavours as a rainbow.
A band of crickets playing their symphony
Under the magical moon.
The clear smell of fresh air,
The benison of crusty bread.
The soft touch of fur as it squeezes through my fingers -
All these have been my loves.

Megan White (10)
Nevill Road Junior School, Bramhall

What Is Green?

What is green? Grapes are green
They huddle up like a team.

What is green? A frog is green
It leaps and sometimes can be seen.

What is green? A tree is green
It stands up like a big machine.

What is green? Grass is green
You'll see it sway in your dream.

What is green? An emerald is green
And it shines, gleams and beams.

Chloé Richards (9)
Nevill Road Junior School, Bramhall

Snowfalls

I was sitting in the classroom,
We were doing poems,
Suddenly, everyone jumped off their seats,
It had started snowing.

Soon it was home time,
The snow lay footprint-free,
Everyone rushed out of school,
When it was twenty-past three.

I went to school the next day,
The snow still lay calm,
I was just about to go in,
When a snowflake fell onto my palm.

I was sitting in the classroom,
We were doing poems,
Everyone sat down again,
For it had stopped snowing.

Beatrix Gough (11)
Nevill Road Junior School, Bramhall

Snake

A slithering snake lies motionless,
Waiting for its prey.
In the shaded grass it halts.
A snake's scale is like mosaic.

The venomous bite is deadly,
The venom slaughters your soul.
Its snapping jaws are fierce like claws,
He swallows his prey, devours the vole.

The snake's rough rattle,
Is the sign of battle.
If disturbed, stay still in fright,
Or you will be the meal tonight.

Luke Harding (11)
Nevill Road Junior School, Bramhall

Shrek

There was an ogre who was smelly,
Who had a rather big belly.
His skin colour was a bright green
And he was very scary and mean.
This ogre was called Shrek,
A name for an ogre who looks a wreck.

The king ordered Shrek,
Who had a spot on his neck
To go and find the king a wife,
Who would be his queen for his whole life.
So Shrek travelled for days and days
And then rested and had a lay.

Shrek saw the princess, very pretty,
Surrounded by lava, such a pity.
To the princess was a bridge
Which was bumpy on its ridge.
On Shrek's journey he had met a donkey,
Who wasn't too keen on crossing a bridge that was wonky.

Shrek crossed the bridge, collected the girl,
Happy to be free, she gave a twirl.
Something magical had happened as the light went dim,
She had turned into an ogre just like him.
They filled each other with fun and laughter,
Happily they lived ugly ever after!

Chloe Belsham (10)
Nevill Road Junior School, Bramhall

Tiger Shark - Cinquain

Tiger
Stripy body
Diving, gliding, floating
Snappy, evil, scary, moody
A shark.

Ciaran Doyle (9)
Nevill Road Junior School, Bramhall

Storm

Storm,
Like God's anger set upon the Earth,
Howling winds whistle through the camp,
Rain, like millions of bullets,
Trying to break through,
Storm.

Storm,
Torchlight forking in the inky black sky,
Mini people in the clouds
Drumming which echoes through the heavens,
Clouds darken,
Storm.

Storm,
People cower below the mighty roar,
Getting more powerful by the dreaded second,
Darkness surrounds me,
Shadows get larger,
Storm.

Storm,
Clouds clear, rain stops,
Drums fade, torches fail,
Shadows withdraw to nothing,
Storm stopped, sun,
Storm.

Scott Thomas (11)
Nevill Road Junior School, Bramhall

Shark - Cinquain

A shark
Eats anything,
Raging, frightening, evil,
Angry, cross, moody and nasty,
A shark.

Lucas Lee (8)
Nevill Road Junior School, Bramhall

Tiger

Great large cats, as well as wild and scary,
Great large cats, as well as orange and hairy,
Creeping quietly in the long grasses,
Everyone hides when he passes,
Except for the ones who do not see him.
Those are the ones who shall be lunch,
Those are the ones who he shall munch.
He silently watches closely,
He watches his prey,
Then as quick as a cheetah he pounces up,
Straight up from where he lay.

When he has eaten he will go to the lake,
In the icy cold water he will have a break.
Round the fields and forests he will roam,
Before he silently crawls back to his home,
Great large cats as well as orange and hairy,
Great large cats as well as wild and scary.

Samantha Clarke (11)
Nevill Road Junior School, Bramhall

Falcon

Gliding, in flight like a weightless plane, hunting,
Hunting, looking from high above, spotting,
Spotting its meal for the day, diving,
Diving, speedily swooping through the air, caught,
Caught the falcon's meal.

Returning, taking the dead animal back to its nest, landing,
Landing where its chicks wait, squabbling,
Squabbling, fighting, they argue for food, playing,
Playing, chicks play while parents rest, sleeping,
Sleeping, resting for the next day's catch.

Liam Shelmerdine (11)
Nevill Road Junior School, Bramhall

The Lunchtime Monster

When you eat your lunch beware,
for lurking in the corridors
a lunchtime monster's there.

At night she cries and stomps her feet,
although she knows she will not eat
until the noon of the next day,
when she eats and eats and eats away.
The lunchtime monster takes your food
then goes and takes another dude's.
She'll crash and smash till one o'clock,
when the clock goes tick-tock
she'll slip away into the attic,
until another day comes back in.

Matthew McCall (11)
Nevill Road Junior School, Bramhall

What Is Green?

What is green? An emerald is green
That was dug up by a machine.

What is green? Grass is green
Swaying in your dream.

What is green? Seaweed is green
Under the sea is where it's seen.

What is green? Cabbage is green
You eat it when it's clean.

What is green? A parrot is green
Sometimes it says things that are mean.

Adam Pickup (9)
Nevill Road Junior School, Bramhall

What Is Red?

What is red? A tomato is red
On a piece of crunchy bread.

What is red? Mars is red
Like a big round head.

What is red? A poppy is red
Across the fields, the seeds they spread.

What is red? Manchester United are red
The best in the Premiership as they said.

What is red? An apple is red
And is sweet and juicy when you go to bed.

George Lee (9)
Nevill Road Junior School, Bramhall

What Is Yellow?

What is yellow? A bumblebee is yellow
And it buzzes in the meadow.

What is yellow? A parrot is yellow
Clever ones say hello.

What is yellow? A gift can be yellow
You give it to your best fellow.

What is yellow? The sun is yellow
The sun creates our shadow.

What is yellow? The Simpsons are yellow
They're on TV and they bellow.

Hannah Rate (10)
Nevill Road Junior School, Bramhall

Night-Time

Stars surrounded by the pitch-black sky
Nothing making a sound, not even a fly
The gloomy trees hanging over the gate
The gleaming moon rising when it gets late
The gushing wind gliding in the air
Two opposite leaves becoming a pair
Dancing together, never apart
And finally resting in a cart
Shining, shimmering in the sky
But now it's time for it to die
For so the moon bowed down to the sun
We know the day has begun.

Aisha Bracewell (10)
Nevill Road Junior School, Bramhall

What Is Green?

What is green? Grass is green
Making up a beautiful scene.

What is green? A recycle bin is green
Turning places nice and clean.

What is green? A grape is green
About the size of a baked bean.

What is green? A kiwi is green
Before it is chopped up in a machine.

What is green? A crocodile is green
Looking extremely serious and mean.

Amy Hollick (10)
Nevill Road Junior School, Bramhall

What Is Red?

What is red? A Ferrari is red
At night-time in its garage bed.

What is red? A strawberry is red
Sitting in its fruit bowl bed.

What is red? Jam is red
On toast and jam it's spread.

What is red? An ant is red
Hurrying swiftly on its treads.

What is red? A brick is red
Harder than a hammering head.

Charlie Kilbride (9)
Nevill Road Junior School, Bramhall

What Is Green?

What is green? A leaf is green,
That has been seen.

What is green? Grass is green,
That is clean.

What is green? Grasshoppers are green,
And they were at the scene.

What is green? Emeralds are green,
That had to go through a machine.

What is green? Caterpillars are green,
And they were eating beans.

Hannah Spencer (9)
Nevill Road Junior School, Bramhall

The Moon

When the evening sun has settled down for the night,
Instead of bright, shiny light,
We see a shade of pastel yellow,
Inside a mellow little fellow.
This little fellow is passing through the sky,
On a bright pastel yellow disc.
It is known that he took a risk of flying into space,
He says it's quite a cheesy place.
You may think he's all alone,
Because you hear him moan and groan.
But when he comes out at night,
The stars are always at his sight.
Not only stars but also clouds,
Thunder, lightning groans aloud.
Now the night has gone so soon,
The sun is up and it's nearly noon.

Jodi Bool (11)
Nevill Road Junior School, Bramhall

Storm

Storm crashing like boulders from the sky,
The soft whisper of rain falling to the ground,
Forks of lightning, dancing like fireworks in the inky black sky,
Rain hitting the roof tiles,
Making them shake and quiver.

Wind whistling down the chimney
Like a howling ghost,
Finally the rain stops and a small beam of light
Appears from the clouds above.

Meagan Moorcroft (11)
Nevill Road Junior School, Bramhall

These I Have Loved

The twinkling radiance of the stars after dusk;
Each one trying to shine brighter than all the rest;
Pure white against the black sky.
The soft, soothing rhythm of the ocean;
Gushing and crashing, tearing up the beach,
Soft juicy texture of fruit; droplets trickling down your chin
Like raindrops dripping down the roof.
Refreshing taste of life.
Warm, deep comfort of fur,
The soft, soft hairs collapsing under your hand,
Seeping through your fingers,
Heavenly aroma of freshly cooked bread,
The nostril-filling scent
That makes your stomach turn somersaults.
Sweet sound of birds at dawn.
These have been my loves.

Olivia Brookes (11)
Nevill Road Junior School, Bramhall

Monsters

Some are big,
Some are small,
Some are very, very tall.

Some are fat,
Some are thin,
Some are smaller than a pin.

Some are green,
Some are red,
Some are even yellow instead.

Some are a mum,
Some are a dad,
Some like my brother are driving me mad.

Jade Imrie (11)
Nevill Road Junior School, Bramhall

I Am The Sea

I am the sea
As big as I can be.

I am the sea
I am not grimy.

I am the sea
I am quite bright.

I am the sea
I am very shallow.

I am the sea
I am very bubbly.

I am the sea
As big as me.

Kirsty Williams (9)
Nevill Road Junior School, Bramhall

Dolphin Couplet Poem

Swimming in the blue ocean
And dancing in slow motion.

Beautiful fast swimmers,
A dolphin's skin glimmers.

Clicking sound to find its lunch,
Lots of fish for it to munch.

Not a fish but a mammal,
Shiny skin but never dull.

Leaping out of the waves,
Always awfully brave.

Natasha Izzard (8)
Nevill Road Junior School, Bramhall

Dogs

A s fast as a river,
B arking thunderously.
C uddly and extremely cute,
D elightful wagging tail.
E xciting competitions to enter,
F etching and catching flying discs.
G reat animals,
H appily playing.
 I mpatiently waiting for their food,
J umping and running frantically.
K ind, fun pets,
L ovely to be with,
M an's best friends.
N aughty little rascals,
O bedient.
P erfect in every way,
Q uite frisky.
R eally fun to be with,
S cruffy and lots of energy.
T ickling their tummies,
U nderstanding the commands.
V ery expensive,
W agging their wonderful tails.
X mas is when they gets presents,
Y apping loudly,
Z ipping everywhere.

Lauren Clarke (11)
Nevill Road Junior School, Bramhall

Summer - Cinquain

Summer
Sunshine, flowers,
Holidays, swimming, beach,
Ice cream, sandcastles, nature, birds,
Long days.

Yolanda Edwards (11)
Nevill Road Junior School, Bramhall

My Books

I have books that are small,
I have books that are tall.

I have books that are light,
Colourful and bright.

I have books that are heavy and thick,
Like the one about the broomstick.

I have books that are blue,
Purple, old and new.

I have books that are red
And about the living and the dead.

I have books by Tony Ross -
The Little Princess is the boss.

I have books by Quentin Blake,
They keep me wide awake.

I have books about the Famous Five -
About the thunderstorm they survive.

I have books about fairy tales
And books about killer whales.

I have books that are small,
I have books that are tall
And I love them all.

Dorothea Christmann (8)
Nevill Road Junior School, Bramhall

Cheetah - Cinquain

Cheetah
Yellow, black spots
Hiding, running, killing,
Eating meat, drinking water, hides,
Pouncing.

Stephen Chamberlain (10)
Nevill Road Junior School, Bramhall

The Mansion On A Mountain

Whoever goes in doesn't come out.
Cobwebs in every corner.
The death of the mother's second daughter,
The ghost of her spirit feels the slaughter
. . . of pain.
Still the murderer has got nothing to gain.
Dead people's bones from trying to get in,
And still people have no sin.
Vandals and dossers trying to get for a dare,
But the dreadful things of which they're aware,
The death of them too would be quite hard to bear.
There's a myth that a graveyard is under the house,
But the entrance to that would be just right for a mouse.
Now right at the front of the mansion just there,
There's a metal barred gate with no reason or care,
The gates were there not only to keep people out, but in as well.
I imagine this place would be worse than Hell,
The mansion was all in darkness, no light, not at all.
If someone stood at the top they'd have a mighty bad fall.
The garden out back, with weeds and dead plants,
You'd think the place would be crawling with ants.
'Oooo' the ghosts say as they hover away.
All this trouble over a tiny little jewel.
People have tried stealing it with loads of different tools.
Right at the top of the tall tower,
Lies a red ruby with masses of power,
As hard as a diamond, as red as roses,
Worth more than anything on this planet.
And that's why everyone wants it.

Natalie Dodd (11)
Nevill Road Junior School, Bramhall

The Horse

The foal was struggling to rise
The wind blew the new mother's mane
Her foal had been a surprise
She was hoping it wouldn't rain
The foal's legs trembled as he tried to stand
And his back was being beaten down on by the sun
A piece of the foal's mane floated away (just a strand)
The foal was reaching up to his mum's tum
Showing he was ready to feed.

Four years had passed since the foal's birth
And at the moment he was galloping round a field
He had been sold (£2,000 he had been worth)
He had been put in a box that had been sealed
Then transported to his new home
Which was near a big grassy park
With a huge field in which to roam.

Now twenty-five and cooped up in a stall
He was remembering his past
As well as staring at a blank wall
He knew this night would be one of his last
Lying down he half-heartedly went to sleep
He knew he wouldn't wake the next day
And that his owners would weep.

Georgina Volp (11)
Nevill Road Junior School, Bramhall

Going To The Beach

Washing your hands after eating mango,
Going to the beach, swimming in the warm sea,
Diving under the water, seeing tropical fish,
Standing on the hot sand.

John Wardle (7)
Nevill Road Junior School, Bramhall

The Night Hunter

She sits there on her perch,
Waiting, waiting, waiting,
And there she does search,
Searching for her meal.

Anything on the ground,
Will never ever hear
Her make a single sound
And still she searches.

At last she spots her meal,
She spreads her wings wide,
To her it does appeal,
Since it is some mice.

When she reaches her meal,
By gliding down upon them,
Then she begins to peel,
Through their warm, red flesh.

With the bodies quite dead,
She carries them to her babies'
Warm, cosy bed,
And then they eat.

Lewis Farrow (11)
Nevill Road Junior School, Bramhall

Tropical Island

I can see the sea's waves
Shimmering in this world,
I can smell the fresh air in this world.
I can feel sand tickling my feet in this world.
I can hear the waves swishing in this world.
I can taste the ice cream melting in this world.
It is very hot in this world.
You can have fun in this world.

Harrison Riley (7)
Nevill Road Junior School, Bramhall

The Storm

At first it was just wind blowing through the grass
like a hairdryer running through your hair.
Then came the rain like tiny blades
jabbing into the Earth's surface.
Next the thunder cried out like your tummy rumbling
but hundreds of times louder.
Suddenly lightning bolts hit trees
like forks stabbing into broccoli.
It was then I decided a storm had begun.

Crashing and raging, the wind took roofs off houses
and pulled trees from the ground.
The rain, determined to overflow the rivers and
flood all the land.
The thunder jumping in at random places,
the lightning making fires,
but then it slowly started to die down
and people came out of their houses.
The dark clouds turned white
and the sun slowly peeped out.
It was then I decided the storm had gone.

Rebecca Doyle (11)
Nevill Road Junior School, Bramhall

A Friendship Simile Poem

A good friend is as warm as a fire.
A good friend is as sweet as sugar.
A good friend is as caring as a nurse.
A good friend is as reliable as the stars.
A good friend is as wise as the three kings.
A good friend is as thoughtful as a priest.
My friend is always there for me.
My friend is as calm as the clouds.
My friend is as funny as a clown.
A good friend is as bright as the moonlight.

Megan Hassell (9)
Nevill Road Junior School, Bramhall

In The Jungle!

The morning sun lights up the flaky,
green growth of the mysterious jungle,
While the tiger prepares for its morning feast.
There all around a never-ending grassy path
leads an explorer to the monkeys'
hang out, way into the jungle's far east.

A great big roar comes from afar,
the king of the jungle wakes,
a great big lion with golden mane,
his fur glistening in the sun.

The leopards prowl around so slowly,
then suddenly, suddenly as quick as lightning
they appear to have gone ahead and run.

Baby cubs play all around while their mothers groom themselves,
but way up high balancing on a tree branch
a ring-tailed coati sits.
And all around in the jungle air
the wild animals play
waiting for the very next sunny jungle day!

Sian Hobson (10)
Nevill Road Junior School, Bramhall

Under The Sea

Down, down in the sea
Deeper than the rocky waves
Where the rock sparkles in the sun
Lighting up the water garden
The big seabed with all its coral
It's like a garden
With flowers and coral, weeds and fern
It has big and small bubbles
And shells on the seabed
It has different sized fishes.

Ross Warburton (9)
Nevill Road Junior School, Bramhall

I Am The Sea

I am the sea,
The mysterious sea,
Dancing, prancing, making tides,
I am the sea.

I am the sea,
The moody sea,
Crashing waves on the shore,
I am the sea.

I am the sea,
The beautiful sea,
My underwater garden grows,
I am the sea.

I am the sea,
The gleaming sea,
A huge glittering mirror,
I am the sea.

Rosie Callan (9)
Nevill Road Junior School, Bramhall

What Is Orange?

What is orange? The great big sun
Giving light so we can have fun.

What is orange? The funny orang-utan
Running away from the scent of man.

What is orange? The tasty orange cream
Its flavour is like a dream.

What is orange? A brilliant clownfish
Moving its tail with a mighty swish.

What is orange? A piece of yummy cheese
It would give the mice wobbly knees.

Daniel Whitaker (10)
Nevill Road Junior School, Bramhall

Granny's Bad Luck

My granny always has bad luck;
I feel sorry for the poor old chuck,
She went to the circus and was hit by a flying clown,
They had her rushed straight into town;
Tossing and turning in the van,
She was dreaming of a holiday and getting a tan;
When she woke up in the hospital bed,
She found she had a big bump on her head.

When she came out of the hospital door;
There was a large puddle on the floor,
Then a lorry came rushing past,
Guess what? The puddle went *splash*.
Poor Granny, soaked from head to toe,
Her heart sank and went very low.
Then she decided to go straight home;
She'd had enough bad luck in one day on its own.

Sebastian Gough (11)
Nevill Road Junior School, Bramhall

Mountains

How beautiful are mountains,
How tall and vast they are,
They look like giant pointed rocks,
When we view them from afar.

The rocky cliffs of mountains,
Covered in crevices,
Are where eagles are roosting;
The jagged rock faces.

The snowy peaks of mountains,
The glaciers and frost,
With all the ice and snow up there,
It's easy to get lost.

Nicholas White (11)
Nevill Road Junior School, Bramhall

These I Have Loved

The sound of the sea like a roaring lion.
The wind whistling outside.
The sight of snow; cotton wool falling from Heaven,
Hailstones bouncing on the roof.
Glass balls smashing as they fall.
The fragrant smell of perfume when someone passes you.
The chemical in the swimming baths.
The feel of sand running through your fingers
And a smooth sheet as soft as silk.
The taste of melted chocolate trickling down your throat.

Natalee Fletcher (10)
Nevill Road Junior School, Bramhall

Tropical Lands

T errific, tremendous, tall trees,
R acing rocky rivers,
O pen oceans,
P erfect palm trees
I cy ice cream,
C reamy carved coconuts,
A mazing animals,
L ovely luscious leaves!

Olivia Farrow (8)
Nevill Road Junior School, Bramhall

Friendship Simile Poem

A good friend is as caring as a nurse.
A good friend is as warm as a bonfire.
A good friend is as pleasant as a cake baking.
A good friend is as fresh as air.
A good friend is a cuddly bear.
A good friend is as cheerful as Christmas Day.

Adam Barker (8)
Nevill Road Junior School, Bramhall

On A Tropical Island

Hear the rain dripping,
Hear the trees swaying,
On a tropical island.

Feel the hot sun,
Feel the leaves brushing past,
On a tropical island.

See the trees and the rain,
See the sun and the leaves,
On a tropical island.

Smell the salty sea,
Smell the creamy coconuts,
On a tropical island.

Amy Mickleburgh (8)
Nevill Road Junior School, Bramhall

I Am The Sea

I am the sea,
Yes, that's me.
My waves are splashing on the beach,
No, I am not a peach.

I am the sea,
Much more than a bee,
Dive over my waves,
Or you can sunbathe.

I am the sea,
Greater than the River Dee,
Float and swim,
But not very dim.

Amar Singh Nijjar (9)
Nevill Road Junior School, Bramhall

Tropical

Hot afternoons and stormy days.
With hot melting ice creams,
Lovely long palm trees.

Hot afternoons and stormy days.
The waves as big as a palm tree.

Hot afternoons and stormy days.
The sand as hot as the sun.

Hot afternoons and stormy days.
With the sun as big as the Earth.

Kelly Crabtree (8)
Nevill Road Junior School, Bramhall

Grenada's Hot!

There's outstanding heat,
And you'll have hot, sweaty feet.
Won't you come for tea?
Oh no! I burnt my knee!
Just take a dip,
Now there's a tip
In the beautiful sparkling sea.

Lea Monk-Steel (7)
Nevill Road Junior School, Bramhall

The Rainforest

The shattering sun beats down.
I feel damp and sweaty.
It's getting dark
I want my auntie Bettie
She will sort the flies out
And take me home for tea.
It will be an occasion just for me.

Noah Miles (7)
Nevill Road Junior School, Bramhall

My Cat

I've got a cat called Charlie,
She's big and fat and cuddly.

I've got a cat called Charlie,
She sleeps on my pillow at night.

I've got a cat called Charlie,
She hides in bags and boxes.

I've got a cat called Charlie,
And I love her loads and loads!

Samantha Kemp (7)
Nevill Road Junior School, Bramhall

On The Beach

Sunny, hot dripping ice cream
Dribbling down your chin.
can you see a drip?
Try and see a little arm
waving from the sea.
Try and come over here
to try and say,
who is up for ice cream?

Nicole Dodd (7)
Nevill Road Junior School, Bramhall

Tropical Poem

I lie in the sun with my children,
Watching the sea flow away,
Looking at a hotel bulletin.
I asked you to stay
Don't go,
Don't go,
Stay on the beach.

Sam Mehta (8)
Nevill Road Junior School, Bramhall

The Sea

See the sea
crashing on the surface.
Coloured garden
right down you go.
There's silence
as the sea slowly calms down.
Everywhere I go
I see fish swimming and swoshing
with glossy bubbles as well.
The sea is as precious
as Heaven's midnight dream.
Sleepy, I wonder why?
Swaying in the distant waves
and glossy shadows waiting to be seen.
With the sea,
sapphire, turquoise and royal blue.
I love to see the sea
as beautiful as me, let's see.

Abigail Swinfield (9)
Nevill Road Junior School, Bramhall

The Big Blue Sea

I am the sea
with my mighty blue waves.

I am the sea
with a scuba-diver swimming in the ocean.

I am the sea
where there's a pufferfish about to explode.

I am the sea
and there's a shark looking for prey.

I am the sea
it's like 'Finding Nemo'.

Sam Corrigan (9)
Nevill Road Junior School, Bramhall

I Am A Dolphin

I am a dolphin, yes that's me.
I live one hundred miles into the sea.
Dolphins have gigantic grins,
I splash other dolphins with my fins.

I like swimming when it's light
Because I don't like it when it's night.
I go out with three dolphins to play.
After all it is a really, really nice day.

I am a dolphin, yes that's me.
I live deep down in deep blue sea.

Darcy Jackson Knight (9)
Nevill Road Junior School, Bramhall

Whale Couplet Poem

I saw a whale under the sea,
hunting for something for its tea.

I saw a whale under the sea,
I want to take it home with me.

I saw a whale under the sea,
eating an octopus for its tea.

I saw a whale under the sea,
the biggest mammal in history.

Alexander Roughley (8)
Nevill Road Junior School, Bramhall

My Tropical Poem

Hearing the waves crashing against the rocks.
Seeing the sun shining down.
Smelling the fresh air.
Feeling the sand beneath me.
Tasting the beautiful ice cream.

Naomi Ball (7)
Nevill Road Junior School, Bramhall

What Is Pink?

(Based on 'What Is Pink?' by Christina Rossetti)

What is pink? A drink is pink
That sits near a sink.

What is pink? A rose is pink
That makes the boys wink.

What is pink? The ink is pink
That was poured down the sink.

What is pink? A scarf is pink
That you wear at the ice rink.

What is pink? My room is pink
There I sit and plan and think.

Logan Gray (9)
Nevill Road Junior School, Bramhall

I Am The Sea

I am the sea,
The mysterious sea,
Shiny as can be,
I am the sea.

I am the sea,
As deep as can be,
It's gleaming like the sun,
But really gooey like a bun.

I am the sea,
As stormy as can be,
Rough like a man,
I am the sea.

Jake Oliver Wyatt (8)
Nevill Road Junior School, Bramhall